THE TRAGIC BRIDE

❧ ❧ ❧ THE STORY OF THE ❧ ❧ ❧
EMPRESS ALEXANDRA OF RUSSIA

THE EMPRESS ALEXANDRA OF RUSSIA

THE TRAGIC BRIDE

THE STORY OF THE EMPRESS ALEXANDRA OF RUSSIA

by

V. POLIAKOFF
(*Augur*)

AUTHOR OF "MOTHER DEAR: THE EMPRESS MARIE OF RUSSIA AND HER TIMES"

NEW YORK LONDON
D. APPLETON AND COMPANY
MCMXXVII

CONTENTS

ILLUSTRATIONS

THE TRAGIC BRIDE

THE STORY OF THE
EMPRESS ALEXANDRA OF RUSSIA

CHAPTER I

THE INCREDIBLE

N an old house of the Rue de Richelieu in Paris there is a small restaurant. The place is, really, one of those crooked passages which in days gone by led to the Palais Royal in the Rue de Montpensier at the back. It is so narrow that the traditional sofa with a continuous row of little tables in front of it has been placed along one of the walls, while the wall opposite is decorated with a long mirror. Near the entrance is the bar, behind which is Madame in a black silk dress with a bit of fur at the neck and wrists. In the floor close to her is a dark hole, from which comes a smell of cooking: it leads to the cellar, where among pots and pans is the domain of Monsieur. The whole place is dark and crusty with age and is filled with appetizing odours especially when the little waiter staggers up through the hole with the dishes. Monsieur is a master of his craft. In his greasy jacket he comes up and walks along the gangway to pass the time of day with his guests. They

I

tell him that his *coq au vin* is delicious, the best they have ever tasted.

On a dark evening in January, 1927, a man strolled into the restaurant. He had been walking about the narrow streets and it was too late to go back to his hotel and to dress for dinner; he would eat in peace in this little place, where he had been before. Madame, enthroned behind the counter, smiled and expressed her pleasure at seeing the gentleman back in Paris; the little waiter drew out a table with a flourish and relieved the visitor of his coat. With a sigh of content the stranger sank down upon the wine-red sofa. Soon a *pichet* of wine stood at his elbow, while from below arose a metallic noise announcing the energetic activities of Monsieur. The place was practically empty; the only other guest that night was a man sitting at a table removed by one from that of the new arrival. The man had evidently dined already for in front of him was a pot of coffee and a glass of liqueur. All was quiet; Madame sat motionless; the waiter had dived into the black hole and the street was empty of traffic. In the expectation of a good meal the stranger enjoyed the restful atmosphere. He settled himself comfortably and his thoughts turned to the book he was writing: the biography of a lovely woman, whose tragic fate in a mysterious way was linked up with racial secrets and behind whose beautiful form stood the shadow of a devilish thing.

Nothing stirred in the narrow passage; a greenish-grey mist had invaded the place and the light of the few electric bulbs shone dull yellow through its layers. The other guest was sitting motionless, pressed against the back of the sofa; he seemed to be asleep; through the haze his face appeared as a pale green mask. It was one of those uncanny moments, when human beings stand on the threshold of things unknown. The mind is nervously alert and a cold shiver of apprehension heralds the approach of unbelievable things. This feeling came over me on that strange night in the restaurant, for I was the man.

The knowledge was suddenly in me that the Eyes were there: two immense eyes lighted from within. They looked at me from the mirror opposite; the glass had dissolved in the grey-green mist and in front of me was limitless space filled with a vaporous substance. Out of it the Eyes were approaching. Were they human? The pupils were enormous and seemed to expand. They were framed as if in a ring of light. Had I seen them before? They were deep as the green sea and piercing as a red-hot point and it was difficult to gaze into them without horror. A lambent flame played through the eyeballs and the expression was sinister. The mist in the mirror became less dense and I discerned a face: yellow, waxen, rigid. The horror increased. The Eyes in the immobile face turned upwards so that only the yellowed ivory of the whites was visible. Death was there! My hands went out in an anguished gesture of defence. The earthenware pot on the table fell on its side, released a torrent of wine and crashed on the floor. This dis-

pelled the terror; in the mirror I saw the reflection of
the luminous bulbs shining dull yellow through the mist.
I looked round; Madame, turned towards me, was
shaking her head in polite reproof; the man at the
other table roused himself as if coming out of a deep
sleep. Our eyes met. Looking him straight in the
face I said mechanically:

"I know you."

He answered with simplicity:

"Yes, certainly."

Then I recognized him indeed. He was the artist,
whose studio in Moscow had been famous for the excellence of its photographic work. My thoughts ran
on like lightning and in a second I knew those eyes
I had seen. On one occasion they had burned into me
like that, but I had forgotten. Now memory came
back in a powerful wave. The eyes were those of
Rasputin.

The photographer and I talked. I did not mention
the strange vision which I had just seen, but spoke
of ordinary things. He told me his tale: destruction
of a home, the fruits of honest labour lost in a moment,
a stand against hardship, cruelty and famine, then
flight. As long as life lasts there is hope and the exile
was building anew a professional career in Paris. I
promised to see him next morning. In fact, I was
anxious to see him again in the hope that daylight
would bring me a sane solution of the strange happenings, which I had just witnessed.

I discovered the photographer next day in a distant suburb, where he had a sort of studio. We talked again of old times. He had been well known and many of the prominent men and beautiful women who made society in Russia so brilliant and so attractive had been his clients.

"While I think of it," said he, "I have somewhere a few plates—all that I have brought away from my collection."

"Do show them to me, I am sure that they will be interesting!"

"All right! I have not looked at them myself since I escaped and I really don't know why I have carried the things with me all this time."

After some searching the photographer produced the plates out of an old cardboard box and delicately, one by one, he held them up against the light. On the first two were the portraits of beautiful women, evidently of the aristocracy, but the dreadful events of the Revolution had played havoc with memory and neither the photographer nor myself was able to recognize them. And then on the next plate I saw the Eyes. It was Rasputin, the man who, by the mysterious power which was in him, ruled the tragic Empress Alexandra and through her the Emperor Nicholas, thus becoming the master of Russia at a dramatic moment in her history. The "Man of God," but in reality the instrument of satanic forces.

"Let me see," said the photographer, "I remember now how this portrait came to be taken. It was in May, 1916. Rasputin was brought to my studio

by a friend. When he entered I said to myself:
'Why, he is a simple peasant!' Then I saw his eyes,
deeply set, of a steely grey colour; there was something heavy about them; when they looked at you,
you felt a material pressure and it was impossible to
look into them for any length of time. I never have
seen other eyes like that. Rasputin was in good
humour, laughed and joked. He said that he wanted
the portraits for the Empress, but insisted on being
photographed also together with the lady who had
brought him. She made me a sign and I clicked the
shutter in pretence. When Rasputin was murdered
his portrait hanging on the wall of my studio fell
down and the glass was broken. A coincidence, naturally; the charwoman confessed afterwards that she
had been clumsy in dusting it, but curious nevertheless."

The portrait discovered in this strange manner is
before me. Rasputin looks through half-closed eye-
lids. A Russian peasant with long hair and uncouth
beard, but what a face, all cut up with lines and ridges,
full of bumps and hollows! He plays with the hairs
of the beard in his accustomed manner. The hand
is gnarled, full of savage force and the fingers could
be talons. He is dressed in the *armjak*—the ordinary
coat of a peasant—but in his case it is of the finest
cloth, lined with rich silk. A sinister figure: the mysterious product of an amazing people, he came out of
space, ran his evil career and went out in a bloody
mist. He had no culture and very little education, yet

by subtle mental processes, which we cannot understand, he penetrated to the heart of things in an
astounding fashion. Physically repulsive and unkempt,
he possessed a strange charm which endeared him to
many people and made him the master of some. Depraved and making no secret of his dissolute life, he,
nevertheless, acquired power over the minds of people
with high principles and a delicate conscience. Unable
to write properly and not having read a single book
in his life, Rasputin spoke utter nonsense and yet,
sometimes, his sayings were clever and proved an
amount of understanding of essential things which
many a highly educated and trained person does not
possess. Rasputin was venal and vain and yet sometimes he refused to do anything for interest and his
penetration of the real motives of people was uncanny. He loved good food, wine and women, yet
there was something ascetic in his nature. Man of
God, or instrument of Satan? The more we study this
amazing human product the more we discover elements
which logically rule out each other but which some-
how manage to survive and to exist together. If Rasputin is the result of a unique confluence of national
characteristics, then we say that next to Lenin the
Russian people were fated to produce in him the most
powerful disruptive agent the world has ever known.
Rasputin and Lenin, each in his own sphere, were
destroyers. The combination of their activities
brought about the Revolution in its peculiar Russian
form.

CHAPTER II

LOVE UNQUENCHED

F people had the courage always to speak the truth many more of the successes and failures of political men would be found to be due to feminine interference. We abstain hypocritically from discussing the influence of sex on politics, yet it remains a powerful factor in life. Social conditions change, but attraction between the sexes retains its power, especially when it is wedded to a spiritual affinity, the presence of which brings the magic word "love" to our lips. In politics the constructive power of love is surpassed only by its capacity to destroy.

The Russian Revolution had to be, but the form it took was the result of love between a man and a woman: Nicholas II, the last Emperor, and the Empress Alexandra, who was Alix, the favourite grandchild of Queen Victoria. Historians agree about the influence which Alexandra wielded over Nicholas; they explain it by her superior will-power. The truth is that the man was enthralled by a passion, which had its source in physical attraction, transformed into deep love and kept fresh by the magnificent devotion of the woman. The will of Alexandra helped her keep secure the position won by her love. As a sovereign Nicholas may be despicable—as the possessor of the jewel of a love shared and ever young he is to be envied.

It was unfortunate for Russia that Alexandra had bred so amazingly true to type. We discover in her the primness, the obstinacy, the aloofness from the world and the attachment to the family ideal with which the biographers of Queen Victoria have made us familiar. Above all, in the Empress Alexandra was the same unquenchable love for her mate. This important characteristic is more marked, if possible, in the Empress than in the Queen. The love of Alexandra for Nicholas became the ruling passion of her life. She was intensely devoted to her unfortunate son and this led her to cause grievous injury to Russia. But the final tragedy showed that she loved Nicholas best. When a Bolshevik Commissar wished to separate the Emperor from his son, the latter was lying prostrate with an attack of bleeding. Alexandra chose to go with her husband. Her love is the key to her influence over him and through him on the affairs of State. The story of the Empress Alexandra—the Tragic Bride—is the story of her love and a love story above all. It is recorded in her letters and in those of her husband, in their diaries and in the evidence of the intimates of their family circle.[1] The Revolution has

---

[1] The letters have been published by the Central Archive in Moscow: *Perepiska Nikolay i Alexandry Romanovikh.*

thrown the shameless light of publicity on the correspondence of Nicholas and Alexandra. The Bolsheviks have published their letters to prove the little mindedness of the last sovereigns and their responsibility for the misfortunes of Russia. But the same materials serve to reconstruct a story of human relations, flowing from a noble sentiment and proving that a crown is no protection against the irresistible drive of fate.

On April 8, 1915,[2] the Empress Alexandra wrote to Nicholas II, who was away at the front:

> *Tsarkoe Selo*
> MY VERY OWN BELOVED HUSBAND,
> Tenderly do my prayers and grateful thoughts, full of very deepest love, linger around you on this dear anniversary. How the years go by! Twenty-one years already! You know: I have kept the grey "Princesse" dress I wore that morning? And I shall wear your dear brooch. Dear me, how much we have lived through together in these years—heavy trials everywhere, but at home, in our nest, bright sunshine!
> Your own old WIFEY

Writing to her from Headquarters on the same day Nicholas said:

> MY PRICELESS DARLING,
> Warmest loving thanks for your dear letter, full of tender words and for the two telegrams. I too think of you on this 21st Anniversary, I

---

[2] The date is in the old style, which in the preceding century was twelve days behind the dates of the ordinary calendar.

Zarskoe Selo.
Aug. 28th 1915.

My beloved Nicky dear,

How can I thank you enough for your very precious — it came as a most welcome surprise. I have reread it already several times & kissed the dear handwriting. You wrote the 25th & I got it 27th before dinner. — All interested us immensely, the children & A. eagerly listened to some parts I read aloud — & to feel that you are at peace fills our hearts with joyful gratitude. God sent you the recompense of your great undertaking — yes, a new responsibility but one particularly dear to y[our] heart, as you are all that

AUTOGRAPH LETTER OF ALEXANDRA FEODOROVNA

wish you health and all that can wish a deeply loving heart, and on my knees I thank you for your love, attachment, friendship and patience, which you have shown through these long years of our married life.

The weather reminds me of the day at Coburg. How sad that we are not together. Nobody remembered that this is the day of our betrothal —curious how people forget quickly. But for them the day has no meaning!

Ever your Huzy, NICKY

Twenty-one years earlier Nicholas wrote in his diary, while at Coburg: [3]

"A wonderful, unforgettable day in my life. This is the day of my betrothal to my dear darling Alix." [4]

For the Russian Easter—April 8, 1916—Nicholas was away from home again and Alexandra wrote:

Tsarkoe Selo

Christ is risen!

MY OWN SWEET NICKY LOVE,

On this our engagement day all my tenderest thoughts are with you, filling my heart with boundless gratitude for the intense love and happiness you have given me ever since that memorable day twenty-one years ago. May God help me to repay you a hundred-fold for all your sweetness.

Yes, verily, I doubt there being such happy wives as I am—such love—trust and devotion

[3] Coburg—capital of the old German Duchy of Saxe-Coburg-Gotha, where the betrothal of Alexandra and Nicholas took place in 1894.

[4] The name Alix was given to her daughter by Princess Alice of Hesse, because the Germans pronounced Alice as Alicée.

as you have shown me these long years with happiness and sorrow. All the anguish, indecision and suffering have been well worth what I received from you, my precious bridegroom and husband. Nowadays one rarely sees such marriages. Your wonderful patience and forgiveness are untold—I can only ask God Almighty on my knees to bless and repay you for everything. He alone can. Thank you, Sweetheart, and feel my longing to be held in your arms, tightly clasped and to relive our beautiful bridal days, which daily brought new tokens of love and sweetness. That dear brooch will be worn to-day! I feel still your grey suit, the smell of it by the window in the Coburg Schloss! How vividly I remember everything! Those sweet kisses, which I had dreamt of and yearned after so many years and which I thought I should never get. You see, as even then, faith and religion play such a strong part in my life. I cannot take this simply—and when I make up my mind, then it is for always. The same in my love and affections. A heart far too big, which eats me up. . . .

These words are a revelation of character. In his letter, which crossed hers, Nicholas says:

MY DEAREST LOVE,

I must begin to-day's letter by remembering what happened twenty-two years ago. I believe there was a concert at Coburg and a Bavarian band played. Poor Uncle Alfred [5] was drowsy

---

[5] Alfred, Duke of Saxe-Coburg-Gotha, second son of Queen Victoria, became Duke after his uncle Ernest, brother of Albert, the Prince Consort.

after dinner and dropped his stick all the time with a bang. Do you remember? This last year we were also separated. It was just before the visit to Galicia. . . .

In the letter of Alexandra, quoted above, there is the sentence: "I love you, my Blue Boy,[6] thirty-one years, and I am yours—twenty-two years."

This is remarkable because in the diary of Nicholas, under the date December 21, 1891, we find:

> In the evening Mamma,[7] Aprak [8] and myself discussed the married life of the young people in society to-day. This conversation irresistibly struck a live chord in my soul. It touched that ideal and the hope which are with me always . . . I want to marry Alice of Hesse. I have loved her for a long time, but more strongly and tenderly since 1889, when she stayed six weeks at St. Petersburg. I have resisted this passion for a long time. I tried to convince myself that fulfilment was impossible. But, after Eddy [9] renounced or was jilted, the only obstacle or abyss, which remains between her and myself, is the question of religion. There is no other obstacle. I am fairly certain that our sentiments are mutual. All is in the hand of God. On His mercy I rely. . . .

So we find a touching confirmation of the thirty-one years of love, mentioned by Alexandra, in the diary of

---

[6] This is an allusion to a favorite book of the Emperor and Empress: *The Boy,* by Marie Corelli.

[7] The Empress Marie Feodorovna.

[8] Countess Obolensky.

[9] Albert Edward, Duke of Clarence, eldest son of the Prince of Wales (King Edward VII) died in 1892.

Nicholas. This carries us back to a time when she was a girl of twelve and he a youth of seventeen. In the Italian Pavilion, in the park of the Peterhoff Palace, near Petrograd, until the Revolution there could be seen a window on a pane of which, cut in with a diamond, were the initials of the two lovers and the year 1884. Love had stolen up to them unawares and had enfolded them in its fragrant embrace. The evidence produced shows that their mutual feeling ran into a deep passion, which stood the test of years. There is other proof in the correspondence—naïvely crude sentences, not meant for a stranger to see, much less to discuss—showing that after twenty years of married bliss physical attraction remained an all-powerful factor between them. Here is the foundation for building the story without recourse to subtle deductions. It will not redound to the glory of the dynasty, but it will protect the reputation of a high-minded woman, whose fate it was to live in a tragic time, which she could not understand and among people by whom she was not understood. The Russians hated her and saw in her the root of their misfortunes. This must not surprise us, because even her own relatives were unable to fathom her true nature.

On September 6, 1915, the Grand Duke Andrey Vladimirovitch mentions in his diary [10] a visit paid by the Empress Alexandra to his mother, the Grand Duchess Marie Pavlovna (Aunt Miechen). He notes

---

[10] *Dnevnik Velikago Kniasya Andreya Vladimirovitcha,* Leningrad, 1925. The Grand Duke was a cousin of the Czar.

that in twenty years, this was the first occasion when Alexandra had come for a private talk, unaccompanied by her husband. Terribly upset by the way things were going on at the front and inside the country, for once she opened her heart.

The Grand Duke remarks:

This episode in our family life is important, because it gave us an opportunity to understand Alix. Her life among us has been enshrouded by an atmosphere of mystery. Behind the veil Alix's personality remained a puzzle. Nobody knew her really, nobody understood her and, therefore, people guessed or imagined things, which in time became merged into various legends. It was difficult to discover the truth. . . . Naturally our talk with Alix cannot restore what has been lost for twenty years. . . . But we have seen her in a new light. We see that many legends are not true and that she stands on the right road. Evidently, her soul overflowed with bitterness and she visited Mamma, because the need of confiding, if only partially, had become overpowering.

The fact of this visit is corroborated in the letter of Alexandra to Nicholas of September third, in which she says:

"Olga, Tatyana [11] and I took tea with Miechen. . . . We spoke much and they looked at things as one ought to; also angry at the fright and cowardice and that none will take any responsibility upon themselves."

Poor shy woman, it was seldom that she could say

---

[11] The two elder daughters of the Empress.

that anybody agreed with her! It was so difficult for her to reveal her thoughts to anybody except her nearest friends, of whom she had few. She relied on her husband to protect her against the world. He was her knight errant. With him away she felt deserted in the world, aware of its cold hate and its judgment which she lacked the power to sway. So widespread has been the condemnation of Empress Alexandra that few have dared to defend her memory and to give the due to her virtues. If ever there was a case in history when fate has used an innocent person as an instrument for destruction it is that of Alexandra. She was the victim of a moral and physical heredity. The tendency of aristocratic families to inbreed allows heredity to play a part in their existence greater than is usual among ordinary mortals. The influence increases with each generation. In addition to inherited mental and moral traits, Alexandra was the carrier of a physical heredity, the fateful intervention of which in the affairs of Russia cannot be overestimated. We mean "bleeding," that mysterious disease, which in some families attacks the males, being transmitted by the females, who externally remain healthy.

In 1574, in the Louvre in Paris, King Charles IX of France, barely twenty years old, was dying of a terrible affliction: blood was oozing from his body through the "pores" and none of the means that Ambroise Paré, the great physician, tried, could stop the deadly flow. So died one of the last Valois, the first royal victim known to history of the fell haemophilia. The disease is characterized by the fact that the blood of the sufferers does not possess the faculty of coagulating. A small cut or abrasion may cause a mortal flow. A blow may produce internal haemorrhage, accompanied by inflammation and excruciating pains. Alexandra's uncle, Leopold,[12] was a victim of it. His sufferings are pathetically described in the letters of his sister Alice, who married Prince Ludwig of Hesse and became the mother of the future Empress.[13] A brother[14] of Alexandra was afflicted in the same manner. And Alexandra's only son, the Czarevitch Alexis, the last of the direct Romanoff line, was a sufferer from the disease. This brought Alexandra under the baleful influence of Rasputin, the "Man of God," who "bewitched the blood" and precipitated the Revolution.

---

[12] Duke of Albany, fourth son of Queen Victoria, born 1870, died in 1884.

[13] Alice, Grand Duchess of Hesse, Princess of Great Britain, *Biographical Sketch and Letters,* London, 1884.

[14] Frederick William, Prince of Hesse, born 1870, killed by a fall out of a window, 1873.

CHAPTER III

SUNNY AND NICKY

HE little Princess of "Hesse and by the Rhine," who was born on June 6, 1872, received from her royal and Imperial god-parents the names of Victoria Alix Helena Louise Beatrice. But her English mother called her Sunny, because she was such a sweet and merry little thing, always smiling, with dark eyes framed in black lashes, a dimple in one cheek and reddish-brown hair. Though the nose was slightly too long it was predicted that she would be a beauty. When she grew up the promise of good looks was fulfilled. At twenty she was a beautiful girl, though shy and reserved. Her face was a striking one, shadowed at times by a sad and pathetic expression. One who came to know her well wrote:

At last, advancing slowly through the masses of greenery came a tall and slender figure. I looked at her, admiration in my heart and in my eyes. I had never imagined her half so fair. And I shall never forget her beauty, as I saw her on that July morning. . . . Her complexion was delicately fair, but when she was excited her cheeks were suffused with a faint flush.

Her hair was reddish-gold, her eyes—those infinitely tragic eyes—were dark blue and her figure was supple as a willow wand. . . . A sweet smile and a world of kindness in her eyes.[1]

Did the mother, with the bonny child at her knee, sense the tragedy which would lurk in these wonderful eyes? For Princess Alice,[2] the second daughter of Queen Victoria, was a woman remarkable in many ways, of which not the least was her uncanny insight into the future. She was highly strung and believed herself to be in contact with things beyond the *visible* plane. Her father, the Prince Consort, to whose memory Queen Victoria, his widow, clung with a desperate tenacity, remained for the daughter a real presence. Princess Alice strained at the leash of physical disabilities, trying to penetrate into what the future had in store for those she loved. In her letters to Queen Victoria there are prophetic passages. The most remarkable is the sentence, which warns German princesses against adopting the Orthodox faith. It occurs in a letter written a few days before the birth of the daughter who was to become Empress of Russia and whose change of religion would be the principal cause of her misfortunes!

Princess Alice was an intelligent woman, of high principles; she believed that "life is meant for work, and not for pleasure." She detested snobbery and

[1] Mme. Lili Dehn, *The Real Tsaritsa*, Thornton Butterworth, 1922.
[2] Princess Alice of Great Britain, born in 1843, died of diphtheria in 1878 after nursing her husband and children. Married in 1862 to Prince (later Grand Duke) Ludwig of Hesse, who died in 1892.

had the courage of her convictions. Far from being a free thinker herself, she respected the views of other people and was not ashamed of her friends. So she allowed the well known philosopher David Strauss to dedicate to her his book on Voltaire. To the court of the diminutive Grand Duchy of Hesse and to Darmstadt, its poky little capital, Princess Alice brought the inspiration of a noble personality. Possessing the rare gift of leadership, she placed herself at the head of a women's movement, which resulted in the creation of medical and charitable institutions far in advance of what existed elsewhere in Germany. The married life of Princess Alice and of her husband, Prince Ludwig (later Grand Duke) of Hesse, was saturated with family affection and interests—the wife brought to the partnership the ennobling influence of her high-minded nature.

The protecting embrace of such a mother would have been invaluable to Alix. Unfortunately, when the child was barely six years old, the mother died. The girl grew up between the father—a good man, but embittered by an irreparable loss and a martinet for discipline, and the grandmother—a paragon of all the virtues, but intensely autocratic. Princess Alix attained womanhood, hungry for human sympathy and not knowing how to obtain it. She had been taught to repress her feelings and to look down upon the world, as if from a pinnacle, which forbade spontaneous movement. A shrewishness was born in her, particularly marked after the marriage of her three elder sisters [3] when Alix remained the only lady at the court of her brother, the Grand Duke of Hesse. It is recorded that a Russian diplomat, discreetly inquiring from the Marshal of the Grand Ducal Court about the character of Princess Alix, was surprised to see the old gentleman get up, close the door and then cautiously whisper that all would be pleased to see Her Highness leave Darmstadt. The Empress Marie Feodorovna, the mother of Nicholas, had had occasion to observe the Princess during the latter's visits to her sister Elizabeth, who in 1884 had been married to the Grand Duke Serge, youngest brother of Alexander III. She thought her nature hard and disliked the idea of such a daughter-in-law. In fact, Marie Feodorovna had another girl in mind for her son: the Princess Helen, daughter of the Comte de Paris, pretender to the French throne, to whom she was related through the wife of her brother, Prince Valdemar of Denmark, Princess Marie of Orleans, his sister.

True love is obstinate and Nicholas, though he did not dare to go against the wishes of his parents, continued to dream of the girl, who had his heart in her keeping. We have described [4] the circumstances connected with the fatal illness of Alexander III, which broke down parental resistance to the match and made

---

[3] Victoria, born 1863, married 1884 to Prince Louis of Battenberg; Elizabeth, born 1864, married 1884 to Grand Duke Serge, brother of Alexander III; Irene, born 1866, married 1888 to Prince Henry, brother of William II.

[4] V. Poliakoff, *Mother Dean: The Empress Marie of Russia and Her Times,* D. Appleton & Co., New York, and Thornton Butterworth, London, 1926.

Nicholas a happy man. Queen Victoria had planned that her grandchild should marry Eddy—Edward, Duke of Clarence, the eldest son of the Prince of Wales—and so become later queen of the United Kingdom. Nicholas alludes to this scheme in his diary. But the Duke was not enthusiastic and the heart of Alix was not free, so the idea was dropped.

Officially the obstacle to a match with the heir to the Russian throne was the difference of religion. Alix refused to accept the Orthodox faith merely for the sake of political convenience. Yet, as she confessed many years later, Alix at the time was deeply in love with Nicholas and "yearned for the kisses which she believed she would never get." The family used its influence to break down her religious scruples. Queen Victoria approved of the match, undoubtedly a brilliant one. But it was Emperor William II who was an insistent and even anxious backer. He hoped that Alix, as a German princess on the Russian throne, would make up for the harm caused to the interests of the Reich by the Danish wife of Alexander III. The brother of Alix—Grand Duke Ernest—was engaged to be married and the presence in Darmstadt of a Grand Duchess would oblige Alix to surrender the position of the first lady in the land. These circumstances and, above all, her love for Nicholas, encouraged Alix to accept the explanations given her in respect to the excellence of Orthodoxy. She wavered and in the spring of 1894 the time was judged ripe for Nicholas to come to press his suit himself. Fortunately we possess the parts of his diary covering this period. The pretext for the visit was the wedding in Coburg of Grand Duke Ernest with "Ducky"—Victoria, the daughter of Alfred, Duke of Saxe-Coburg-Gotha.[5] Nicholas was sent to represent his father, the Emperor, at the ceremony. He was accompanied by an uncle, the Grand Duke Vladimir and by the latter's wife, Marie Pavlovna.[6] This is Nicholas' own description of these momentous days in his life:

> *April 4th,*[7] *Monday* . . . half an hour before arrival we donned our uniforms and at 5 o'clock ran in to Coburg station. Quite a gathering to meet us: Uncle Alfred, Aunt Marie, Alix, Ernie, Missy,[8] Ducky and other less exalted personages. A guard of honour from the local battalion of the 95th regiment. After the march past of the latter and the presentation of several people, we got into carriages and drove to the Schloss, where we found excellent accommodation. In the street the Bürgermeister [9] welcomed us with a gracious

[5] The second son of Queen Victoria, Duke of Edinburgh. His wife was Marie, Grand Duchess of Russia, sister of Alexander III and, therefore, aunt of Nicholas. "Ducky's" marriage was not successful, she was divorced and married the Grand Duke Cyril, a cousin of Nicholas, and now pretender to the Russian throne.

[6] She was a princess of Mecklenburg-Strelitz, known in the family as Aunt Miechen. It is in connexion with her marriage that the prophetic words about the danger of changing religions were written by Princess Alice.

[7] Students of history deprived of the possibility of seeing the original documents in the State Archive in Moscow, will find much interest in a Berlin publication: *Dnievnik Imperatora Nikolaja II,* Slovo, 1923, with extracts from the diary of Nicholas II.

[8] Marie, born 1875, daughter of Grand Duke Alfred, married 1893 to Ferdinand Hohenzollern, who became in 1914, after the death of his uncle, King Carol, King of Roumania. Queen Marie of Roumania.

[9] Mayor of the town.

speech. The people gave us a good reception; perhaps, the new Treaty with Germany has something to do with this.[10] We unpacked and at 7:30 went across to Uncle Alfred and Aunt Marie to attend a family dinner in their pleasant home. Then we walked to the theatre, where was presented an excellent operetta: Vogelhändler. We sat up after with Aunt Marie and returned home at midnight.

April 5th, Tuesday. Oh God! What a day! After coffee, about 10 o'clock we came to Aunt Ella [11] to the rooms of Ernie and Alix. She is more beautiful than ever, but so sad! I was left alone with her; the talk took place for which I longed so long and so much. The conversation lasted until 12 o'clock, but without any result, because she resists the change of religion. Poor thing! She cried a great deal. We parted in a quieter mood. Lunched with Aunt Marie. Then with Auntie Ella and Uncle Serge I drove to pay a visit to the Grand-Duchess Dowager, a sister of Aunt Olga Feodorovna.[12] She has a pretty castle just outside the town. We also visited Philipp of Coburg and his wife.[13] It rained hard up to 3 o'clock. Went for a walk with Uncle Vladimir towards the old castle on the hill. Queen Victoria arrived at 4:30 in pomp: half a squadron of her Dragoons of the Guard before and as many behind her open carriage and a whole bat-

---

[10] A Russo-German commercial treaty very advantageous to Germany, had just been signed.

[11] Grand Duchess Elizabeth, wife of Serge Alexandrovitch, elder sister of Alix, murdered by the Bolsheviks in 1918.

[12] Grand Duchess and famous beauty.

[13] Father of King Ferdinand of Bulgaria, married to Princess Clementine of Orleans.

talion as guard of honour. These marched past her in the square at the salute with Uncle Alfred leading them. We all in full uniform looked on from the windows of her apartments. Having paid our respects we dispersed to our rooms for tea. By arrangement one-half of the family dined with her at 9 o'clock and the remainder at Aunt Marie's at 7 o'clock. Went to the theatre; a comic play: "Das Stiftungsfest." Sat for a time in the billiard room and then went home. The day has left me morally exhausted.

April 6th, Wednesday. I got up early and went for a walk with Uncle Vladimir at 8:15 in the direction of the old castle on the hill. It serves now as Museum for ancient weapons. Returned at 9:30 and had coffee all together in the common drawing room. Alice came and we talked again. I avoided as much as possible the subject we discussed yesterday; I am content that she consents to see me and speak to me. At 12 o'clock we went to lunch with Aunt Marie. The rest were obliged to wait for the Queen until 2 o'clock. After some dawdling we went in two carriages to Rosenau, a place which belongs to Uncle Alfred. . . . On the way back we met the Empress Frederick [14] and Beatrice. [15] All got out and started kissing in the middle of the road. Donned Prussian uniform and went to the station to welcome William. [16] He arrived at 6 o'clock and has also taken up his residence at

---

[14] The Princess Royal, eldest daughter of Queen Victoria, widow of the Emperor Frederick and mother of William II.

[15] Daughter of Queen Victoria, married to Prince Henry of Battenberg. Her daughter Victoria Eugenie is the wife of Alphonso XIII, King of Spain.

[16] William II, German Emperor.

the Castle. At 8 o'clock a family dinner, after which there was a short performance upstairs. Two small plays were performed very well on a miniature stage in one of the drawing rooms. After tea all retired to their rooms. William sat up with us until one o'clock.

April 7th, Thursday. Wedding day of Ducky and Ernie. I got into trouble being half-an-hour late for breakfast at Aunt Marie's, where the whole family had assembled. I was obliged to cross the square all alone at a run. At 12 o'clock we met in the Hall upstairs. After the signature of the civil marriage contract we went to church. The service was short. Ernie and Ducky are a fine pair. The pastor preached a fine sermon, the contents of which amazingly fitted the problem, which now faces me. At that minute I had a violent desire to look into the soul of Alix! After the wedding—a family dinner, and at 3:30 the young couple left for Darmstadt. I took a walk with Uncle Vladimir. We climbed at last to the Castle and inspected in detail the Museum. We had just come back, when the storm broke and rain fell through the night. Because of the Emperor, who does not wear civilian clothes, we put on uniform for the dinner at Aunt Marie's. Afterwards we went, that is we ran across, to the theatre. They presented the first part of Pagliacci and a good play. Beer and champagne were served in the billiard room.

April 8th, Friday. A wonderful, an unforgettable day in my life. The day of my betrothal with my dear darling Alix. After 10 o'clock she came to Aunt Miechen's. We talked and all was clear between us. Oh God! A mountain has been lifted from my shoulders. What joy to gladden the hearts of dear Papa and Mamma. I went about all day dazed. I could not believe that all this had happened to me. William sat in the next room with the aunts and uncles, awaiting the result of our talk. Alix and I immediately went to the Queen and then to Aunt Marie, where in their joy the family indulged in an orgy of kissing. After lunch we went to Aunt Marie's church [17] and had a thanksgiving service. Then off to Rosenau, where there was a ball . . . dancing not interesting me, I walked about and sat with my fiancée. We returned home at 6:30. Already there was a heap of telegrams. Dined at 8 o'clock, drove about to see the illuminations and then went upstairs to attend the State Concert. Brilliant music by the string band of the Bavarian regiment. The rest of the evening we remained in our drawing room.

April 9th, Saturday. In the morning the Dragoons of the Queen executed a musical programme under my windows. Very touching! At 10 o'clock came darling Alix. We went together to the Queen to have coffee. The weather was cold and the day was grey, but my soul was brimming over with joy and light. At 11:30 Uncle Bertie [18] insisted that the whole family should be photographed together in the garden. I sat after lunch in Alix's room answering telegrams. We drove together in the pony-cart to Rosenau. I held the reins. Wonderful. . . .

---

[17] The Duchess of Edinburgh had remained in the Orthodox faith upon her marriage and possessed her private chapel and priest.

[18] Edward, Prince of Wales, eldest son of Queen Victoria, later King Edward VII.

The Tragic Bride

April 11th, Monday . . . the attitude of Alix towards me has undergone a complete change and I am in heaven. This morning she wrote two sentences in Russian without a single mistake. . . .

April 12th, Tuesday . . . at 10 o'clock went with Alix to the Queen for coffee; I must now call the Queen—Granny. . . .

But everything has an end and a few days later Nicholas and Alix had to part. Queen Victoria took the girl away to Windsor, while Nicholas returned to Russia to join his parents, who were impatient to hear from him the details of his wonderful love affair. The separation from Alix was to be for a few weeks only, but to Nicholas it seemed that all joy had departed from his life. We shall avail ourselves of the interval to look at the young man with whom Alix was now head over heels in love and who was destined to become monarch of a great empire.

Officially described in Russia as a Romanoff, Nicholas, really, was of German descent, for the Empress Elizabeth, a daughter of Peter the Great, had adopted as heir the son of her sister Anna, who had been married to a duke of Holstein-Gottorp, a princeling on the Danish border. This youth became the Emperor Peter III, dethroned and murdered by his wife, Sophie-Frederica of Anhalt-Zerbst, better known to history as Empress Catherine II, the Great. Their son—Paul I—is the ancestor of the Romanoff family, representatives of which occupied the Imperial

28

throne until the Russian Revolution of 1917. The legitimacy of Paul is contested so that the Romanoffs may have a few drops of Russian blood in their veins after all. But, if heredity counts for anything, Nicholas was a Hesse, even more than Alix herself. She at least through her mother, the Princess Alice, daughter of Queen Victoria, claimed Saxe-Coburg and Guelph descent. But both the parents of Nicholas had more than fifty per cent of Hessian blood. Alexander III, the father, was a son of Maximilienne (Marie Alexandrovna) a Princess of Hesse of the Grand Ducal House. There was Hessian blood also on the maternal side, for Princess Dagmar of Denmark, the mother (Marie Feodorovna), was the daughter of Louise, of the line of Hessian Landgraves and had for paternal grandmother Princess Louise Caroline of Hesse. The pedigree of Alexis, the son of Nicholas and Alix—the last czarevitch—shows this relationship clearly. It also shows that Nicholas and Alix through a common grandfather (Louis II of Hesse) were cousins in the second degree: not only were they of the same blood, but they were closely related by direct descent. In view of intermarriage in preceding generations and of the known existence of a hereditary inclination to disease, there was much to be said against the match. But we doubt if eugenic considerations were the cause of the originally unfavourable attitude of the parents of Nicholas towards his love affair. His mother, Marie Feodorovna, disliked the aloofness she sensed in Alix. It is possible

also that she was influenced in her judgment by her
sister Alexandra, Princess of Wales, who knew the
girl intimately, having had occasion to watch her during her long residences at the British Court. Nicholas,
blindly in love, certainly never gave a thought to anything of the sort. He could not have done so because,
being an ordinary man with a mediocre education and
with a restricted outlook, questions of eugenics were
beyond his understanding.

Justice is represented blindfolded, but Cupid should
strut about with a magnifying glass screwed into one
eye and a patch over the other. For there is no limit
to the amazing capacity of lovers to exaggerate pleasing qualities and to ignore defects in the object of their
devotion. Men and women alike are untrustworthy
witnesses as to exact fact, but people in love by their
misstatements become a public danger. In this respect the lover is even more dangerous than the historian, who has an axe to grind. In the letters of
Alix, Nicholas appears not as he was, but as she saw
him in her imagination: a handsome man with a commanding presence; a noble nature and a heart of gold;
a great prince—the leader of an adoring nation; a well
of wisdom overflowing with virtue. He was all this
to her and more! If anybody had dared to hint that
her lover was an ordinary young man, the speaker
would have been forever in her bad books.

Yet Nicholas was an ordinary young man. He was
not handsome, though in his eyes there lurked the
charm for which his mother was famous. Of a height

below the average, with a slight figure and with a
carriage suggesting meekness rather than majesty,
Nicholas did not look the ideal prince. His nature
was not bad and his outlook upon the world was kindly,
but of especially noble sentiments he had none. If
others ever thought of him as a great ruler, he himself did not share that view: of power he had the
instinctive fear of the man who hates responsibility
and lacks the spirit to command. He was not a fool,
but he neither showed the desire, nor possessed the
capacity, of acquiring knowledge. His childhood had
been passed in the gloomy palace in which his father
had elected to seek refuge from assassins. Thanks to
Mr. Heath, the English tutor, his originally frail
body had been strengthened by physical exercise and
teachers had hammered into him the rudiments of a
secondary school curriculum. He learnt to speak English and French fluently and knew the rules of good
society. But all this was no real preparation for the
hard task of government. When later, as a young
officer, he became more independent, his society was
limited to that of a few irresponsibles and gay grand
dukes and men of "good" families. The serious duties
laid upon him by his father bored him and he tried to
avoid them whenever possible. Innumerable small
details in his diary of that period show that he did
not do anything particularly wicked, but certainly nothing intelligent or useful. He led the empty life of an
officer in the guards and we find in his diary the
pleasures of the bottle mentioned often but an inter-

esting book or an instructive conversation, practically never. The love for Alix came early and, no doubt, was a powerful influence. It did not prevent him from carrying on the usual intrigues with the ladies of the Imperial *corps de ballet*. On the whole, a colourless young man. An expert on Russia said of him:[19]

Who was he? What was he? He was a very ordinary young man, neither very stupid, nor very clever, not ill disposed, not devoid of a sense of humour, and certainly not without charm. He might have been a very fair Guard's officer; or one could imagine him as a private country gentleman living a tolerably happy life in the management of his estate, dabbling in rural politics and travelling abroad in the long summer holidays. He had an agreeable manner, he would have been popular among his friends, and the defects of his character would have attracted slight notice. . . . But he was the heir of the Romanoffs and there was an intolerable burden upon him. This little man, who had no glint of imagination, was endowed or believed himself to be endowed with absolute power. He accepted the legend with a wooden, stubborn faith, that forbade further inquiry. . . . He had an unintelligent sense of duty and his desire was to keep the autocratic tradition intact.

It was not the fault of Nicholas that he was like that. He fitted exactly into the frame of a spineless period in Russian history, when, under the deadening influence of the rule of his father, Alexander III,

---

[19] Dr. Harold Williams, Foreign Editor of the *Times* and for many years correspondent of the *Daily Chronicle* at St. Petersburg: *New Europe,* August 1, 1918.

national life was stamped with mediocrity. It was a time of little men with tin virtues and petty vices, of men stupidly mean, with stunted brains and with tightly laced hearts; a period, when even villains turned out to be only thieves in a small way. Russia was steeped in a soulless meanness and, when the Revolution came in the days of Nicholas II, it was found that there were no statesmen left, nor even were there any sensible revolutionaries. There was a morass through which the hideous menace of Bolshevism was burrowing its slimy way.

If in the possession of retrospective knowledge we may attempt to judge men who are no more, and a period which is closed, the future remained a closed book for Nicholas. He certainly did not give it a moment's consideration, when under the spell of his love, he returned from Coburg to Russia to join his parents. In his heart was the hymn of love and he was full of a passionate desire to see his engagement cut down to the shortest limit compatible with court etiquette, so that he and Alix should be united as quickly as possible and for ever. But the wedding of an exalted person—the heir to the Imperial Throne of All the Russias—was a State affair, needing careful and long preparation. When a month later the impatient bridegroom left for England to join his financée at Windsor, nothing definite had been settled.

CHAPTER IV

UNDER GRANNY'S WING

HERE was no pleasure for Nicholas in the prospect of passing a month at Windsor under the eagle eye of formidable Granny, but he was overwhelmed with joy at the thought of seeing Alix. Travelling in the *Polar Star,* the fine Imperial yacht, he set out for England in state, as befitted the heir to a great throne. The story of the visit is told in his diary and is full of piquant details of the intimate life at the English Court.

The course of love, running smoothly, can be traced in the daily inscriptions. We note the growing intimacy between the lovers; Princess Alix is interested in the diary of her beloved Nicky; she takes it away and writes in it sentimental verses in the approved Victorian style. There are moments when she is quite the simpering fräulein. A note of intense feeling runs through her remarks; we read pieces of wisdom—forerunners of the influence which she will exercise later in married life. A motherliness and a sense of spiritual superiority are in evidence, throwing light on future relations. In this respect the words written by Alix on July twentieth are arresting. Evi-

34

'dently Nicholas had confessed some of his youthful peccadilloes, among them his intrigue with a young ballet dancer. Alix's comments are on a high moral plane, tinged with religious feeling. But youth will not be denied and often we see the lovers in a playful mood: the nicknames of *Spitzbube* and *Lausbube*[1] could not have been used with gravity. Between the lines we sense kisses snatched behind the back of Granny and read of hours whiled away in a blissful contemplation of each other.

In the diary Nicholas does not appear as a great man, not even as an intelligent man, yet there is no doubt about the sincerity of his love for Alix. In the extracts given further on the inscriptions made by Alix are in italics. If the names which he mentions most were counted, it would be found that the word Frogmore comes first on the list. The unceasing repetition shows the place held by the memory of the Prince Consort in the heart of Queen Victoria. The Royal Mausoleum at Frogmore was the centre around which the life of the Royal widow gravitated.

June 20th,[2] *Wednesday.* At 6:30 A. M. we sighted the Galloper lighthouse and turned into the estuary of the Thames. A cool breeze blew from the shores of England and it was a grey morning. At 10:30 we entered the Thames and began to ascend without a pilot. The *Thunderer*

---

[1] German slang words, the meaning of which is approximately: saucy and roguish knave.

[2] In this chapter the dates are given in the Gregorian style to facilitate comparison with contemporary English sources.

—ironclad—and the fortress in Sheerness saluted, hoisting our naval flag. . . . A special train flew with me to London; at Waterloo Junction I saw Staal.[3] Ludwig[4] came into the saloon and I parted with Dymka.[5] Twenty-five minutes later I arrived at Walton and at 3 I met dear Alix. I found again the joy from which I had been parted in Coburg. It is nice to live, the four of us, in the little house of Victoria and Ludwig. The rain poured and we passed the remainder of the day indoors. We dined alone at 8 o'clock.

June 21st, Thursday. I slept splendidly in my comfortable little room. How happy was I, when I woke in the morning and remembered that I am living under one roof with my darling Alix. . . .

June 22nd, Friday. Another wonderful and quiet day. The same as yesterday. Verily life in paradise! . . . The whole morning I was with my Alix in the garden, sitting on the old path under the chestnuts; she worked and I read to her the "Matelot" of Loti. . . .

June 23rd, Saturday. To my regret it was necessary to pack up and leave the free life at Elm Grove (Walton). The whole morning until lunch, we sat with dear Alix and I read to her. At 4 o'clock Victoria, Alix, Ludwig and myself drove in the Royal carriage and four to Windsor, which we reached in an hour. . . . Dinner was at 9 o'clock. We were fourteen. Kneebreeches were worn; my shoes were awfully tight. Dear

---

[3] Baron von Staal—Russian Ambassador at the Court of St. James.
[4] Prince Louis of Battenberg, husband of Victoria, eldest sister of Alix, British Naval Service.
[5] Prince Dimistry Golitzin, Major-General, attached to the person of Nicholas.

Alix and I passed a wonderful evening together.

June 24th, Sunday. I got up at 8:30. The weather was splendid. Had coffee in my room and at 10 o'clock drove with Granny and Alix to Frogmore for breakfast. At 11—in the mausoleum —Divine Service, which I liked very much. . . . Yesterday at 10 in the evening a son [6] was born to George [7] and May. General rejoicings and delight.

June 25th, Monday. In the morning we drove with Granny and Alix to Frogmore for breakfast. Then I sat with my fiancée in the garden, taking full advantage of the summer weather. We drove together and returned home towards 1 o'clock. Lunched at 2 and in great ceremony went in an open carriage to fetch Granny from Bagshot, where live Uncle Arthur [8] and his wife. We had tea in a tent. Went over his fine house and saw the Indian room. Returned with Granny. The great rhododendron bushes amazed me. Dined at 9:30. For the first time I put on my Windsor coat with red collar and wristbands. Then I sat in dear Alix's room.

June 26th, Tuesday. The weather was stuffy. At 10 o'clock, as usual, we went to Frogmore for breakfast. I walked a little with Alix near the Lake. At 4:45 we proceeded by train to Richmond and from there in carriages to White

---

[6] Edward Albert, Prince of Wales.

[7] George V, born 1865, second son of King Edward VII and Queen Alexandra, eldest daughter of King Christian IX of Denmark; married 1893 to Victoria May, born 1863, daughter of the Duke of Teck— Queen Mary.

[8] Prince Arthur, Duke of Connaught, third son of Queen Victoria, born 1850, married 1879 to Princess Louise of Prussia, who died in 1917.

Lodge, where Georgie and May are living at present. I was very glad to see them. He showed us his newborn son. Aunt Alix, Victoria and Maud also arrived. We left at 7, the weather being extremely stuffy and dark, but no rain. Dinner was quite small. In the evening I sat with my dear Alix.

June 28th, Thursday. I got up early, had coffee with my dear Alix and took leave of her for one and half day. At 8 I left for Sandringham by special train accompanied by Dymka G. and Colonel Byng.[9] Arrived with the sun shining wonderfully bright at 11:15 and was met by Aunt Alix, Victoria and Maud. By a pretty road through young pine plantations we drove to their house and saw Uncle Bertie. At 12:30 we went in large company to Kings Lynn to be present at the sale by auction of the horses from Uncle Bertie's stud. First we entered an immense pavilion, in which some 200 farmers sat with their families, devouring a lunch, of which we also partook, sitting at a separate table on a platform, as if it were a stage. The sale of fifty horses lasted an awful length of time. In the beginning things were livelier; I bought two mares with their colts. This occasioned an *"enthusiasme indescriptible."* Then it turned cold and I felt the draught. Returning home we had tea and went into the garden. The wind carried a mist from the sea. We inspected the stables, the kennels and other buildings. The rooms in the house are remarkably well furnished. We dined at 9; then we played bowls and smoked downstairs. I

---

[9] Honourable Henry Byng, Equerry in Waiting to Queen Victoria, attached to the person of Nicholas during the latter's visit to England.

missed Alix very much. Indeed, I felt depressed.

June 29th, Friday. The morning was wonderful when I awoke; after my bath I had coffee with Uncle Bertie in his room downstairs. He left at 10 for London. I remained with Aunt Alix and the cousins; went for a walk with them; we had a look at what we had not seen yesterday. I visited the pastor in their old church, Probyn,[10] the stud of thoroughbreds and the hothouse. I looked at the room of poor Eddy. We lunched at 11:30. I planted a tree in the garden and at 3 we left for the station. The heat and the dust in the train were indescribable. I was filled with delight at the thought of meeting Alix. Even such a short parting with her seems too long. The Archduke Francis Ferdinand[11] arrived in the evening. In his honour there was a big dinner with music and uniforms. Great perspiration!

June 30th, Saturday. In the morning I paid a visit to the Archduke, who had been left all alone in the castle until 12. Granny, Alix and I drove to Frogmore for coffee. Then we two went to Cumberland Lodge to see Snipe[12] and her sister. It was indescribably hot. Before lunch I read and wrote. The children of Lyko[13] and Aunt Beatrice were impossible at table, so that even Granny became angry. At 4 arrived Victoria and Ludwig. Alix sat in my room. We all had tea in Frogmore, and then drove about

---

[10] Sir Dighton Probyn, Equerry, Keeper of the Private Purse, then Controller of the Household. Died 1926.

[11] Heir to the Austro-Hungarian throne. His murder in Serajevo in 1914 precipitated the Great War.

[12] Princess Helena Victoria, eldest daughter of Princess Christian.

[13] Prince Henry of Battenberg, Governor of the Isle of Wight.

separately. The dinner was a small one and we
had music in the porch.

July 2nd, Monday. At 1 the whole family
living at Windsor, Granny excepted, left for
London direct for Marlborough House to attend
a large family lunch. We were thirty sitting
at three tables. I remained until 5 upstairs
with Alix in the rooms of Victoria and Maud.
Their rooms reminded me of last year. At 5
I drove with Victoria and Ludwig to Clarence
House for Aunt Marie's garden party. Fortunately it cooled off towards evening. I saw
J. I. Shahovskoy [14] and the officers of the *Polar
Star.* At 6:30 I left for Windsor with Alix, the
Duchess of Albany [15] and her daughter. I was
glad at the prospect of remaining again alone
with my dear fiancée. Sandra [16] has arrived for
two days. We dined at 9:15 and then had music
downstairs.

> *Hush, my dear, lie still and slumber,*
> *Holy angels guard thy bed.*
> *Heavenly blessings without number*
> *Gently falling on thy head.*
> *Better, better every day.*

July 3rd, Tuesday. At 8 went riding with
Sandra, Miss Hood [17] and Dymka; what a pity
that dear Alix cannot ride yet with us as she has

[14] Prince Jakov Ivanovitch Shahovskoy, Commander of the *Polar
Star.*
[15] *Nee* Helena, Princess of Waldeck, married 1882, to Duke of
Albany. Their daughter Alice, born 1883, married to Duke of Athlone,
brother of Queen Mary, in 1904.
[16] Alexandra, Princess of Saxe-Coburg-Gotha, granddaughter of
Queen Victoria.
[17] The Honourable Rosa Hood.

Y. Crabra. Aug. 25.
1915.

My own beloved darling
Sunny,
Thank God it is all over
and here I am with this new
heavy responsibility on my
shoulders! But God's will be
fulfilled — I feel so calm,
a sort of feeling after the
Holy Communion!
The whole morning of that
memorable day Aug. 23, while
coming here, I prayed much
& read your first letter over
& over again. The nearer

AUTOGRAPH LETTER OF NICHOLAS II

just finished her cure and the pain in the legs endures. We galloped across the fields like mad. Returned home at 9:30. At 10:15 drove to Frogmore: then sat with Alix near the ruins and read the newspapers, whilst she did needlework. We returned home at 12 to see Janysheff.[18] To lunch, the Duchess of Albany, who afterwards left. Aunt Marie arrived at 5. Went with Alix and Sandra in the carriage to meet Granny on the Eastern Terrace, where 1,000 boys, future sailors, executed gymnastic drill to the accompaniment of music. They then marched past. They are from Greenwich school. We had tea at Frogmore and drove about all three. We laughed a great deal telling each other funny stories. The evening was wonderful and much cooler than the preceding ones. We dined at 9:15 with a few guests. Then there was music downstairs. Uncle Alfred came to my room for a smoke and drank two or three glasses of Pilsner. I was deprived of the extra half hour, which I could have passed with my darling Alix. What is written below is by her hand. I am deeply touched—she wrote it in my room.

With unending true devotion better far than I can say.[19]

July 5th, Thursday. At 8 I rode with Aunt Beatrice to the end of Queen Anne's Ride. We came back bathed in perspiration at 9:30. Had tea with Granny at Frogmore and then quickly

---

[18] Archpriest of the Winter Palace Church. Was sent to instruct Alix in the Orthodox faith.

[19] These same words are repeated, placed in quotation marks, twenty-one years later in a letter of the Empress of December 12, 1915.

returned with Alix to the Castle to leave for a one day's stay in London. At 1 we left Windsor and went straight to Marlborough House. It was amusing and at the same time delicious to sit with my dear Alix in the train [*many loving kisses*] and to drive as we liked through the town, though Gretchen [20] and Byng were with us in the carriage. It was very hot. At 2 we lunched with Aunt Alix, Victoria and Maud. I was glad to be with them even a short time. At 5 we five drove to Louisa's [21] and McDuff, where we had tea. We saw their children—two little daughters. Dined at 7:45 and then went to the Gaiety Theatre, to see the famous play: "Madame Sans Gêne." The French players were divine. Returned at 11:30 and supped with Aunt Alix. I sat up with my dear fiancée until 1 o'clock.

July 6th, Friday. I awoke at 9:30 and had my bath in the same corner bathroom on the roof. Four of us had coffee: Alix, Victoria, Maud and myself. After breakfast we went down to Aunt Alix, where Victoria received her birthday presents. It is a curious coincidence that for the second year running I am in England with them at this time. I sat with my Alix and wrote letters home. To lunch came Uncle Bertie, Georgie, Louisa and McDuff. The heat—pyramidal! After lunch the two girls gave a sort of performance [*God bless you my angel:*] one played the violin and the other danced—a Spanish dance

---

[20] Fräulein Margarete von Fabrice, in waiting on Princess Alix.
[21] Princess Louise, Princess Royal, eldest daughter of King Edward VII, born 1867, married 1889 to Alexander Duff, First Duke of Fife; their daughters: Lady Alexandra, born 1891, married Arthur, Prince of Connaught, 1913, and Lady Maud, born 1893, married Lord Carnegie, 1923.

42

with the tambourine. Aunt Marie came to say goodbye: she is leaving for Rosenau. We were dying from the heat and, as usual, waited wearily for the time to leave. With the 5 o'clock we left for Windsor; to travel together with my dear Alix is for me an intense joy. From the station we went straight to Frogmore for tea; Granny came soon after. The heat was suffocating and a squall drove everybody indoors. We returned to the Castle, whilst it began to pour. At 8:45 dinner, a family affair, with the fat aunts and their husbands. At 10 we adjourned to the Waterloo Hall, where for three hours we listened to "Philemon and Baucis" and the "Navarraise," an entirely new opera of Massenet. After this there was supper standing, but not before each male and female guest had passed (before the Queen) kissing hands. I sat with Alix and went to bed with the dawn.

July 8th, Sunday. I have become extremely lazy and cannot make up my mind to write home, though I should give them my news. Every hour with darling Alix is dear to me and I regret to lose it. The weather has become overcast and it rains. At 5 arrived the Empress Eugénie [22] with her nephew Napoleon, who last winter was in St. Petersburg. Granny received them in the "Queen's Closet," the same in which last year I was invested with the Garter. After tea with Alix started with her for Cumberland Lodge to visit the family of old Christian.[23] We talked a lot and on the way back were caught in the rain.

---

[22] Widow of Napoleon III.
[23] Prince of Schlesvig Holstein, married 1866 Princess Helena, daughter of Queen Victoria (Princess Christian) born 1846.

Dined at 9. I sat next to the Empress. Conversation until 11 o'clock. This implied standing and prevented smoking. I felt thoroughly exhausted.

July 10th, Tuesday. The weather is cooler. At times it rained. At 10 to Frogmore. I walked alongside Granny's ponycart. Then I sat with my [*for ever and ever*] Alix and returned with her to the Castle at 1 o'clock. To lunch arrived Aunt Beatrice and Lyko. Received a telegram from dear Mamma from Abo. At 5:30 in spite of the rain we went to Frogmore and had tea in the house and then drove through Eton and Slough: Alix and I alone in the closed carriage. At 9 sat down to dinner with several very noble lords and their ladies. There was music. After food there was endless conversation standing. I passed a wonderful long evening with my Alix.

July 11th, Wednesday. After lunch I got into my Hussars uniform and at 4:15 we went by train to Aldershot. Uncle Arthur and his staff met us at Farnborough Station and an escort of Inniskilling Dragoons accompanied the Royal carriage during the drive through the camp. The troops are here in barracks, huts and tents. About 6 we arrived at a one-storied wooden house, like a bungalow in India. My room is on the same corridor with all the Aunts and Alix. We were very

Es muss was Wunderbares sein
Ums Lieben zweier Seelen,
Sich schliessen gans einander ein
Und nie ein Wort verhehlen!

44

Under Granny's Wing

Und Freud und Leid und Gluck und Not
So mit einander tragen,
Vom ersten Kuss biss in den Tod
Sich nur von Liebe sagen!

much afraid that they would separate us. We
had tea with Granny, dawdled in the garden and
admired the view. Alix and I sat together before
dinner. I put on the uniform of the Imperial
Circassian Escort. The generals of the garrison
were invited to dine. At 10 we walked down to
see the Military Tattoo; Granny arrived with
the Aunts and Alix. In the darkness, lit by the
torches, four composite bands marched past with
guards of honour representing the four nations
of the United Kingdom: then they united. The
musical programme was very well executed. We
returned at midnight, the air was cold and dank.
I sat a while with dear Alix, though one can hear
all through the partitions.

July 12th, Thursday. I slept remarkably well,
waking at 9 o'clock, when Alix called to me from
the garden through the window to come to
breakfast with Granny. The weather was mid-
dling, cloudy, but the sun came out at times. I
donned full Hussars uniform and at 10:45 we followed the Royal carriage on horseback to the
parade ground. In all there were about 10,000
troops. After the Royal Salute the march past
began: first the Mounted Artillery, then the
Cavalry, Foot Artillery and Infantry. The last
passed a second time in brigade column. The
cavalry—at the trot and then at the gallop. I
admired the horses and the smartness of the
horsed batteries. The Scottish infantry is fine in

45

kilts. The review ended with a general advance to the flank and with the Anthem. We rode to the station. The rain began to fall fast. At 5:30 we went to Frogmore for tea and from there I drove with Alix in the pony carriage. The evening was clear and warm. At 8 I drove in uniform to the Horse Guards to [*all is well that ends well*] dine in the officers' mess. Everything was simple and without ceremony. Talked until 11:30. On my return went to dear Alix with whom I passed a wonderful hour.

> *That his peace may tend you,*
> *And his love caress you,*
> *Is the wish I send you*
> *In the words: God bless you.*

July 14th, Saturday. I did not ride in the morning as I was very sleepy. At 10 went to Frogmore. It was hot, at times thunder was to be heard. The Duke de Némours [24] lunched with us, a Frenchman of olden days. At 5 o'clock I went with Alix in the pony carriage to Cumberland Lodge, where we had tea. M. Wolf played the violin:

> *La nuit j'aime être assise*
> *Être assise en songeant,*
> *L'œil sur la mer profonde,*
> *Tandis que pale et blonde*
> *La lune ouvre dans l'onde*
> *Son éventail d'argent.*
> (*Victor Hugo*)

The accompaniment was played first by Snipe and then by Alix. Aunt Helena showed me her

---

[24] 1814–1896, second son of King Louis-Philippe of France.

rooms upstairs. We left at 6:30. I with a
headache. Lay in Alix's room, trying to sleep.
Dinner at 9 o'clock. There was a small concert
in the drawing room. Singing by Mlle. Calvé,
Plançon and Alvarès. All three are equally
famous. They executed the programme marvellously. Granny gave presents to all three. We
went to our rooms at 11:45. I sat with my Alix.

July 15th, Sunday. Dinner at 9:15, only Court
officials. Little Lord Playfair, Lord in Waiting,
mistook me for the Windsor curate and brought
me up to the Queen, which caused all those present
to laugh merrily and long. I sat with dear
Alix.

July 16th, Monday. Rain in the morning until
9 o'clock. I could not ride with Aunt Beatrice
and wrote and worked in my room. At 10 I went
for a walk with her; we reached Frogmore,
when Granny and Alix drove up. Lunch was
somewhat earlier and at 3:30, in a pouring rain,
we drove to Richmond [*My own precious one,
God bless and protect you and never may you forget her, whose most earnest desire and prayer is
to make you happy.*] where an official reception
awaited us. Crowds of people in the streets and
an escort of the 8th Hussars. At 5 at White
Lodge, in the presence of the whole family, took
place the christening of the little son of Georgie
and May. Granny gave him seven names.
Among others I too stood godfather. Instead of
immersing the child the Archbishop [of Canter-
bury] wetted his finger and drew it in a circle
around his head. Then we had tea in a tent in
the garden. Four generations were photographed
in a group. On the way back there was no rain.

An officer nearly came to grief because his horse stumbled. We arrived in Windsor at 7 :45 *Lausbube*. Dinner was late and the evening ended at 11 o'clock. I sat with *Spitzbube* a long while.

July 17th, Tuesday. After coffee with dear Alix I went to the station to say goodbye in London to Aunt Alix. I returned to Windsor in time for lunch. A strong wind. Prince Shahovskoy reported from Cowes by telegraph his arrival there.

Es giebt Tage und Momente, die Strahlen werfen konnen über Jahre! April 20th Easternight! Shall we ever forget it, oh my kind sweet Mannykins! [Here a heart is drawn with the words inside : toi, toi, toi, toi.]

At 3 o'clock we passed into the drawing room; the brothers Reszke sang. Two jewellers were camping in my room. I bought a trinket from each. Had tea in Frogmore and drove about for a long time. So long that I began to feel cold. On the way back we stopped near the chapel, where Eddy is buried and Granny ordered Alix to put a wreath on his tomb. After dinner there was again a concert. Selected melodies from the new opera "Signa" were sung—a weak colourless composition by the Englishman Cowen. I had a wonderful evening with my delicious fiancée. I am dying from love for her!

July 18th, Wednesday. Georgie came to lunch. He and Alix sat in my rooms with me—I added the words "with me" because otherwise it sounded strange. The weather has improved, there was less wind and the clouds have gone. At 6 o'clock we went to Frogmore; had tea in the pavilion with Aunt Helena, Thora and Louis.

Before driving we looked at the cows and dogs
from which Granny took leave. We came home
at 8. A quiet dinner; only the household. There
was music. In the evening I sat with Alix.

*I dreamt that I was loved, I woke and found it
true and thanked God on my knees for it. True
love is the gift which God has given—daily
stronger, deeper, fuller, purer.*

July 19th, Thursday. [*Hourrah.*] This was
written by my darling Alix in her joy that I am
remaining two days longer. Even this is good,
for, originally, I was to leave on the Saturday.
Had coffee with Granny and at 10:15 left Windsor. In the train we two were parted. The
ladies were in one carriage and Lyko and I in
another. At 12:40 we reached Portsmouth in
a downpour. We went aboard a small yacht, the
Alberta, and our luggage having been brought
over, we proceeded along the beautiful Sound
towards the Isle of Wight. A salute was fired
by the cruisers in Spithead roads. The *Polar
Star* swinging at a buoy in all her beauty vis-à-vis
Cowes, followed suit. At the landing stage we
got into carriages and drove straight to Osborne.
I lived here 21 years ago and it is curious that I
can remember next to nothing about it. [*Sweety
dear.*] I like the house and the situation very
much. The view from the windows on the Sound
and towards the other side is extraordinarily
pretty. After lunch I made myself comfortable
in the rooms downstairs; Alix is on the floor
above. We went over the house and the new
Annexe with the Indian room. Then we went to
the seashore where, like a child, I paddled about
with naked feet. We returned in the pony car-

riage and dined at 9, but the evening dragged on until 11. Sat with Alix.

July 20th, Friday. Granny's existence here is an exact replica of Windsor. For us it is different, because of the sea.

My own boysy dear, never changing, always true. Have confidence and faith in your girlie dear, who loves more deeply and devotedly, than she ever can say. Words are too poor to express my love and admiration and respect—what is past, is past, and will never return and we can look back on it with calm. We are all tempted in this world and when we are young we cannot always fight and hold our own against temptation, but as long as we repent and come back to the good and on to the straight path, God forgives us.

"If we confess our sins, He is faithful and just to forgive us our sin." God pardons those who confess their faults. Forgive my writing so much, but I want you to be quite sure of my love for you and that I love you even more since you told me that little story, your confidence in me touched me, oh, so deeply, and I pray to God that I may always show myself worthy of it.

God bless you, beloved Nicky dear.

After coffee in a wooden pavilion exactly like that at Frogmore, we went to look at the hothouse. The weather was overcast, but warm.

July 21st, Saturday. In the morning it rained and we had breakfast in the dining room. I was photographed in [*The clock is striking in the belfry tower and warns us of the fleeting hour, but neither heeds the time which upwards glides. For time may pass away but love abides, I feel*

*his kisses on my fever'd brow; If we must part,
oh! why should it be now? Is this a dream?
Then waking would be pain, oh do not wake me,
let me dream again!*] the garden. At 1 P.M.
Aunt Beatrice, Alix, Thora and I went in the
steam launch to see the start for the race. There
was a fair wind; Lyko led in his [*only a word—
I wrote so much on the other side—Love*] yacht,
but the prize was awarded to another gentleman.
We came home for lunch. The weather improved. Drove with Alix to the orchard, where
we ate fruit. Then went over the Osborne and
Albert Cottages. I can't remember anything of
our stay there in 1873. Had tea at 6 and then
waited very long for Granny to come out—it is
intolerable to sit with hands folded and always
to wait without end. At last, at 7:30, the three
of us went into the island to the town of Newport. On the way back we en- [*There is a little
word in every language dear, in English 'tis
forget me not, in French 'tis souvenir*] countered
three of our officers, who were taking a walk.
Dined at 9 and I passed a wonderful evening with
my dear darling Alix.

July 22nd, Sunday. . . . Our sailors walked in
the garden and were presented to Granny, who
greeted them; they lined up on the terrace.
Drove with Alix in the pony carriage to the
shore; we sat on the sand and watched the tide.
Our officers came to dinner; I presented them
to Granny. I passed my last [*Ever true and
ever loving, faithful, pure and strong as death*]
evening with my fiancée.

July 23rd, Monday. A sad day—parting—
after more than a month of delicious life in

Paradise. In the morning it rained and then a
mist arose. To have a longer day Alix and I had
coffee together at 9 o'clock and then came down
to breakfast at 10 o'clock. We were again photographed. First I with my suite—Dymka and
Col. Byng, then I with dear Alix in the drawing
room. About 12 we drove with her and Snipe
into Cowes crossing [*Love is caught, I have
bound his wings, love. No longer will he roam
and fly away, within our two hearts forever
love sings*] the river Medina by ferry. We went
into a shop, where they make enamelled flags
for pins and brooches. Ordered two trinkets for
Alix. Went out in the steam launch into the
roads and then to Osborne Bay where we took a
boat, because the launch got on to a sandbank
near the landing stage. Lunch at 2. Our sadness grew as the moment of parting came nearer.
I did not leave even for a minute the side of my
dear darling [*Sweet Nicky love*] fiancée. With
Granny and her we went after tea for the last
time for a drive in the direction of the town of
Ryde. Dinner was a little earlier than 9 o'clock
and the band of the Marines from Portsmouth
played. I bade good-bye to the ladies, the gentlemen and to the Munshy;[25] changed into
naval uniform, said good-bye to kind Granny and
drove to the landing stage with Alix and Lyko.
I parted from my precious darling and was rowed
away in the gig. On the *Polar Star* I found a
long, wonderful letter from Alix [*never forget
your own true Spitzbube, who loves you so
deeply*] which she had given to Radzig. I was
deeply touched. Sent her an answer by Byng. The

[25] Teacher of Hindu language to the Queen.

sadness and longing have made me feel faint.
Janysheff and Mr. Heath were already on board.
God grant that we meet again in joy and good
health. But this cannot be soon. In about two
months.

While the *Polar Star,* increasing speed, proceeded
up the Channel, homeward bound, Nicholas tried to
find consolation by reading the words which Alix
had written in advance in the pages of his diary:

> *Fidèle toujours l'attendre,*
> *Toujours l'aimer, ouvrir les*
> *bras et toujours les lui*
> *tendre. Sur cette page*
> *blanche que ne puis-je*
> *y graver un seul mot:*
> *le bonheur!*

CHAPTER V

HE lovers had agreed to meet again in September at the Grand Ducal Castle of Wolfsgarten near Darmstadt, where Alix was to stay while completing her instruction in the Orthodox faith. Back in Russia Nicholas counted the days which separated him from that happy moment of reunion. The fatal illness of his father upset his plans. The blow fell when Nicholas was packing to leave for Germany. The celebrated Professor Leyden, called in by the anxious Empress Marie Feodorovna, had found Alexander III ill beyond all hope of recovery. As a last resort the patient was ordered to go south to the mild climate of the Crimea.[1] Nicholas, who was not told the whole truth about the deadly nature of the illness of his father, was torn between filial affection and a passionate desire to see Alix.

The whole day [says he in his diary] the sense of duty, which compelled me to accompany my

---

[1] For the tragic circumstances of this medical consultation see *Mother Dear: The Empress Marie of Russia and Her Times,* Chapter XVI.

parents to the Crimea, fought with the violent desire to fly to darling Alix in Wolfsgarten.

Duty won the day: all my plans are changed and
I have had to write about all this to Alix.

Nicholas goes with his parents because it is his duty,
while his heart is with his future wife.

Writing to Alix and receiving letters from her had
become the great joy of Nicholas. The post in Russia, even for the Imperial family, was not too punc-
tual and days passed without news from Darmstadt.
Then Nicholas moped and tried to find consolation
in reading the sentences written by his beloved into
the pages of his diary. So on September eighteenth
—a day without news from Alix—he read "God bless
you, my own precious one. Many tender kisses" and
his thoughts turned to her with delight. Afterwards
a batch of letters arrived and Nicholas overflowed
with joy. Among these letters was one voicing her
grief at the prolonged separation. In the palace on
the cliff, high above the blue waves of the southern
sea, while Alexander III was fighting death, his son
walked in the beautiful grounds or sat on the boulders of the seashore, torn between anxiety for a beloved father and longing for the girl of his heart. His
agitation could not remain a secret from his parents
and Alexander III decided to see Alix and to bless
the future wife of his son. Nicholas records his feelings, when he was told to invite his fiancée to come:

Papa and Mamma have consented that I should
ask dear Alix to come here. . . . Their loving

wish to see her makes me indescribably happy. What a joy to meet again so unexpectedly, but it is sad that this should be due to the present unfortunate circumstances.

The telegraph got busy and Grand Duchess Elizabeth, the sister of Alix, left Moscow for the frontier to meet and accompany the bride of the heir to the throne. For five long days Nicholas did not know what to do with himself; he tried to find an occupation in attending to the arrangement of the rooms destined to harbour his beloved Alix. His excitement became uncontrollable, when she telegraphed from the frontier asking to be received into the Orthodox faith without delay. At last on October tenth she came to him, his Alix!

The quickest way for the traveller to reach the southern shore of the Crimean peninsula is to leave the train, which brings him from the north, and to follow the carriage road, leading from the town of Simferopol into the mountains. Soon the giant Tchatyr-Dagh—the tallest peak of the chain, seen from afar, as the train rolls up across the flat steppe, is hidden from view by the maze of the foothills. The eye accustomed to the flat monotony of the Russian plains is pleasantly attracted by the infinite variety of hill and dale, which closes in from all sides. By the side of a swift river, which soon becomes a mountain torrent, the road winds snakily upwards. A luxuriant vegetation is everywhere. Great trees form beautiful groups on the ridges; some of the hills have a dark green cap of dense forest, while others stand out in naked relief in cold shades of white and pink. Grasses carpet the valleys with luscious green and, in places, flowers cover the ground so thickly that the meadows are enamelled in blue and red and yellow. Crystal-clear brooks and rivulets bubble and tortuously flow down the hillside round boulders covered with bright mosses. The road winds up and up. Stately oaks and tall chestnuts give pride of place to great pines and there is coolness in the air, for we are near to the top of the pass, where for about a mile the road runs across a flat moor with a stunted vegetation. Suddenly the traveller feels the warm breath of sweet air on his face: the welcome of that earthly paradise, which is the southern shore of the Crimea.

Aeons ago the high volcanic chain, which bordered the south-eastern edge of the Crimean peninsula began to crumble into the deep sea at its foot. An undercliff was gradually formed as a ledge about one hundred miles long and from two to six miles broad. New volcanic outbursts cut through it, throwing up rocks and strewing about gigantic boulders. To this was added the gnawing action of numberless torrents. The undercliff was transformed into a maze of deep canyons, twisting valleys and curiously shaped hills, hillocks and crags. Protected by the mountains from the cold wind of the north, the place enjoyed an exceptionally warm climate, which, combined with abundant water, produced a luxuriant subtropical vegetation. Coming from the bleak north over the pass we have described, the traveller enters a wonderful country: vineyards, orchards, plantations of fig trees, pomegranates and almonds, brightly flowered bushes, gardens, rich with flowers, are on all sides. In the background are densely wooded hills, while in front, far beneath, is the dark blue sea, sparkling in the vivid sunlight. The traveller may be somewhere in Tuscany for all he knows; certainly it is not Russia. No wonder that after Russia with its windswept plains, frozen in winter, parched in summer, the southern Crimea appears like God's own land, paradise on earth.

In this delightful place Nicholas waited for his Alix at the foot of the pass where the road branches off along the coast towards Livadia. The sky, the sea and the air itself on this wonderfully warm and calm day seemed to be of the divinest blue. The air was laden with scent from the gardens and plantations. From the picturesque white villages on the multi-coloured hillside the natives streamed on to the road to present the bread and salt of welcome to the travellers, or to offer garlands of flowers and baskets of fruit. Laughing, shouting children threw clouds of bright blossoms over the young pair. The carriage became a bower of greenery. Driving through the scented countryside with Alix at his side, her hand in his and her shoulder touching his own, Nicholas thought that he was in heaven.

Oh God [confided he to his diary] what a joy to have her here at home, quite close to me—the burden of sorrow and trouble on my shoulders is already lightened by half.

In a cloud of white dust the high-stepping horses swept the carriage up to the porch of the palace in Livadia. A guard of honour presented arms to the future Empress and Nicholas led her by the hand up the staircase to the room of Alexander III. Nicholas was suffocated with emotion and Alix, what with the strain of travelling and shyness, was pale as death. Marie Feodorovna met them on the threshold. Her marvellous dark eyes held those of her future daughter-in-law. With a sudden gesture, she raised her arms and putting them round the neck of the stately Alix drew her down into a motherly embrace. Then, taking each by the hand, she led them up to the sick Emperor, who was reclining in his armchair; an imposing figure, but the emaciated face foretold the fatal end. The children sank down on their knees. Raising his great hand he placed it on the head of Alix and then slowly made the sign of the cross above her, conveying to her his fatherly blessing. In a weak voice he bade her welcome and expressed the hope that she would be a good wife to his son. Marie Feodorovna beckoned to them to leave the sick room as the patient was visibly affected by the interview. Before taking Alix to her rooms Nicholas entered with her the palace church, where a thanksgiving service was held to celebrate her safe arrival.

In the diary of Nicholas, small details faithfully recorded show the hold of Alix over him. He positively could not live away from her. During these terrible days of the last illness of Alexander III they were together all the time. Nicholas, attached to his father, as he undoubtedly was, felt the presence of death, hovering in the shadow, with painful keenness. But love was there, too, not to be denied, so that behind the tears lurked the smile of undeniable happiness: a mixture repulsive to contemplate, if it were not so palpably free of self-consciousness. Even when working on the affairs of State, which Alexander III now passed on to him, Nicholas wanted to be near Alix and brought the papers to her room. While he puzzled painfully over the maze of business she sat next to him, embroidering a covering for the chalice, to be used on the day when she would partake of Holy Communion according to the Orthodox rite. From time to time Nicholas put away the dull documents and assisted, as he says, in the work of embroidering. He went for long walks and drives with Alix to favourite places on the shore and in the hills. We discover that at the time already her health was none too good and Nicholas mentions his constant anxiety that she should not overtire or get again the pains in her legs for which she had just taken a cure.

From time to time, Nicholas was called away to see his father, to speak with his mother, to meet members of the family or to discuss current affairs with ministers and Court officials. As a hostage for his swift return to the adored presence he left his diary on the table of Alix. Her thoughts were also with him and about him; she did not wait always for his return to express them, but wrote them down, as they came, into the book. These inscriptions are of great interest, not only because they show her true nature, but because they throw light on future events. On October fifteenth, she writes:

Sweet child, pray to God. He will comfort you. Don't feel too low. He will help you in your trouble. Your Sunny is praying for you and the beloved patient.

And again on the same day we find a piece of advice—the forerunner of a definite view on the position of Nicholas as autocrat:

Darling boysy, me loves you, oh so very tenderly and deeply. Be firm and make the doctors, Leyden or the others, come alone to you every day and tell you how they find him, and exactly what they wish him to do so that you are the first always to know. You can help in persuading him then too, to do what is right. And if the Doctor has any wishes or needs anything, make him come direct to you. Don't let others be put first and you left out. You are father dear's son and must be told all and be asked about everything. Show your own mind and don't let others forget what you are. Forgive me, lovey.

We possess scores of letters of the Empress Alexandra to her husband written more than twenty years later, at the height of her influence over him in political affairs. But the note quoted above sums up exactly the views which we find in her voluminous correspondence. Religion already played an important part in their lives. On October sixteenth Nicholas records that he prayed together with Alix. She adds:

> *I have been able to pray with you in Church for your Darling Father. What a comfort—you near me, all seems easier and I know you will always help me. God be with you, my soul.*
>
> *Sweetest darling, God bless you. He is near you, and Sunny also in her thoughts, so Sweetykins must never feel lonely.*

And on the next day:

> *Tell me everything, my soul. You can fully trust me, look upon me as a bit of yourself. Let your joys and sorrows be mine, so that we may ever draw nearer together. My sweet one, how I love you, darling treasure, my very own one.*
>
> *My soul, when you feel low and sad, come to Sunny and she will try to comfort you and like her namesake warm you with her rays, God helping.*

But serious thoughts and even the presence of death do not prevent the joy of living peeping playfully round the corner and at the end of the same page we read:

> *Only yours, quite yours, your very own little Spitzbube! Pussy mine!*

As the days passed it became apparent that the end of Alexander III was very near and Nicholas devoutly says: "Our only reliance and hope is in the mercy of God: let His will be done."

And Alix to show her sympathy writes down:

Angels guard thee day and night and Sunny
prays earnestly for your happiness.
May love and peace and blessing without end
Wreathe all your path like flowers, O my friend,
And if a thorn should touch you where they grow
Believe, indeed, I would not have it so.

On October twentieth Nicholas notes in his diary:

My God, my God, what a day. The Almighty
has called to Him our adored, dear and deeply
loved Papa. My head is going round. . . . He
died like a saint. Oh, God help us in these sad
days. Poor dear Mamma. In the evening we had
Prayers for the Dead in the same bedroom. I felt
as if I too were dead. The pain in the legs of
Alix has returned.

So at this tragic moment Alix remained near to his
thoughts. We must not be too hard on the young man
for allowing his love affair to cut into his bereavement.
Alix was the supreme mistress, who owned him body
and soul. On the preceding evening during the religious ceremony she stood near him, immovable and
pale as marble. The Russians looked at her statuesque
beauty with awe and the whisper went round: "She
is the Funeral Bride." Tragic events encouraged
superstitious people to say that the omens for the
future were unfavourable. Poor Tragic Bride, life
had in store for her many misfortunes, which she
could not foresee and, if she had been able to do so,

63

it is doubtful if that would have made any difference, for she was very much in love. And she firmly believed that her lover was destined to be a great, good and glorious monarch. In justice to Nicholas it can be said that he did not share this illusion. The exalted adoration of Alix made him the happiest of men, but he had also an overpowering sense of his insufficiency for the Imperial throne. He knew that "the worst possible thing had happened" to him: "the thing which he had feared all his life," but "the Almighty had given him as a reward happiness, of which he had not dared even to dream—God had given him Alix."

Alexander III was dead and Nicholas was proclaimed Emperor; the members of the Imperial family and the people present at Court immediately took the oath of allegiance to the new sovereign. But of this we fail to find a single word in his diary. For his mind was completely taken up with the thought of Alix. On October twenty-first, the first day of his reign the Emperor sets down:

> "In our deep sorrow the Almighty has given us the light of a deep joy: at 10 o'clock in the presence of the family my dear darling Alix was anointed with the Holy Oils and after the service we partook of Holy Communion together with her, Mother Dear and Ella. Alix read the Responses and prayers in a wonderfully clear and distinct voice.

On the next day we find Marie Feodorovna and the family discussing with Nicholas the arrangements for

From an Old Engraving

PRINCESS ALICE, DAUGHTER OF QUEEN VICTORIA
AND MOTHER OF ALEXANDRA FEODOROVNA

MARIE FEODOROVNA, MOTHER OF NICHOLAS II

his wedding. His personal feeling and that of his mother was that the ceremony should take place forthwith, while Alexander III "was yet under the roof of the house." Other members of the family protested against this privacy and insisted that the marriage should take place with due pomp in St. Petersburg after the funeral. There is a callousness about this discussion which is surprising, but it is explained not only by the demands of a rigid etiquette, but also by the Russian fatalism which deprives death of a great deal of the horror with which it is viewed in other countries. The family won its point and it was decided to postpone the wedding ceremony until after Alexander III had been laid to rest with his ancestors in the Cathedral of the fortress of St. Peter and St. Paul. A few days later the sorrowful pilgrimage across the whole of Russia began. Nicholas and Alix travelled with the widowed Empress in the special train, which slowly carried Alexander III towards his last resting place. In Moscow the coffin was taken out and brought in procession to the ancient cathedrals in the Kremlin, where it was exposed to the adoration of the multitude for a whole day and night. Marie Feodorovna in her grief preferred to be with her beloved sister Alexandra, Princess of Wales, who had hurried from England to the Crimea as soon as news of the approaching death of Alexander III had reached her. Nicholas and Alix were left very much to themselves and passed every moment they could during the train journey together. The noble traits in the character of Alix must have been of great assistance to her in those days to establish her moral ascendancy over Nicholas. The sentences interpolated by her into his diary are illuminating:

Gott geht mit dir Seinem Kinde, fürchte dich nicht

Auf jedem Punkte, wo du stehst, ist ein Schutzengel.

Wo du bist is dein Gott, wo dein Gott ist, da ist ein Helfer. (October 27)

All can vanish—only not thy God and thy loving heart.

Bear thy burden with firmness and hope. God gives thee strength to bear, as surely as he lays the burden on you. God crowns thy patience as soon as He takes the burden from thee.

Ask yourself often: how should I act, if I perceived the angels, who are witnesses of the most invisible deeds. (October 31)

Your most secret tears are known unto God, He loves them.

Make work your pleasure—then your peace will be joy.

Suffer, bear, spare, save, pardon, but always love. (November 1)

God will be ever near you and watch over you and will comfort you in your sorrow. He alone can, when others fail thee.

Wheresoever you may be, your God is with you and your heart, and it is His pleasure to listen to all voices. Das eben ist der Liebe

Queen of Love

Zaubermacht dass sie veredelt, was ihr Hauch beruhrt.

Various are the ways God leads you, sometimes the road is even, sometimes steep; nevertheless He never forsakes you, but keeps His friendly guiding hand over you, and the further He leads you the more you see that the term of our voyage is: perfection, blessedness, freedom.

(November 3)

Love, however low it may speak, speaks yet distinctly to thy heart, love's accent is a voice from the light of Heaven. Love is earnest and joyous, forbearing and vigorous. Death cannot shatter love. Love's silence is beautiful and sweeter often than words. What love unites no human hand can separate, Love will one day unite all loving ones. *(November 5)*

What took Nicholas' breath away was that this noble and divinely beautiful creature, full of goodness and wisdom, who treated all people with such cool reserve, came to life in his arms and under his kisses became a tender lovesick girl. He was her slave. The amount of affection of which a human being is capable is limited. Henceforward the Empress Marie, his mother, would have to surrender the exclusive position she had held in his heart and to share it with Alix. To share is an optimistic expression for it is easy to guess who of the two women had the better chance; the mother remains the wise adviser and confidante, but Alix is the undisputed mistress of the heart of Nicholas.

67

The Tragic Bride

Poor Nicholas in spite of his love had a difficult time during the days before and after the funeral of his father. The town was full of kings and princes, who had arrived to be present at the ceremony of the burial. The Emperor William II, the Kings of Denmark and Serbia, the Prince and Princess of Wales and a score of less important royalties had to be met at the station, escorted to the Palace and granted private audiences. There were also deputations from foreign regiments, of which Alexander III had been the honorary chief and delegations from corporate bodies, of which he had been president or patron. All these people had to be treated according to the rules of strict etiquette. Then there were the affairs of State, of which the young Emperor understood little, but which could not wait. There were audiences to grand dukes, to ministers and generals, interviews with the Master of Ceremonies and Marshal of the Court. Nicholas had to find time for the tedious ceremonies and duties, while his heart begrudged every minute which kept him away from Alix, the incomparable, the beloved, the only one!

Nicholas came to hate the people, who prevented him from devoting all his time to his bride. The King of Serbia and the Prince of Roumania, whom he received with affability in private audiences and who were reluctant to break off the charming conversation, little suspected the hard words Nicholas set down later about them in his diary. He even "hated" his aunt, the beloved sister of his mother, the Princess of Wales, because she took up his time too. "I hope she will not remain long now" confides he to his diary. But he became calm when Alix laid her cool hand on his brow and spoke words of devotion and love:

> *Sweet angel, God bless you. My love grows ever stronger and deeper for you, my very own precious soul. I cannot express in words what I feel for you, but, darling, you know my tender sympathy, having myself shortly gone through the same sorrow and without a mother. But we have not lost our dear ones, they have only gone before, and are waiting for us. It is a comfort to try and live and act as they would have wished and to try and follow in their footsteps. They are near us, I am sure, and love us deeply. Your duties are many and hard ones too, and may God give thee strength to bear and fulfil them—let her, who will, God grant, be soon your little wife, share all with you, joy and sorrow.*
>
> *(November 8)*

Here we take leave of Alix, for, when she joined the Orthodox Church, she became Alexandra Feodorovna, and as such she has passed into history. Only once does her old name appear in an official document; it is her marriage contract, which was signed on November 11, three days before the wedding. The Minister for Foreign Affairs, Giers, and Prince Worontzoff-Dashkoff, Minister of the Court, representing the Emperor, and General von Werder, representing the Princess "of Hesse and by the Rhine," signed a document wonderfully engrossed on parch-

69

ment and behung with seals by which Nicholas recognized having received with his bride a magnificent dowry (this was naturally a fiction because the House of Hesse could not boast of worldly goods), which was to remain her personal undivided property and also, in the case of her survival, she was assured of a rich widow's portion. There were many other clauses, paragraphs and remarks in the document over which the notaries had worked for a long time. But Nicholas and Alix cared little for it; the only contract they cared for was a kiss.

CHAPTER VI

FULFILMENT

HE broad avenue, filled with humanity so that footpaths and roadway are indistinguishable, appears from above like a black river, flowing slowly through a canyon, the sides of which are palaces and mansions. Lateral streets pour in new masses, causing eddies and crosscurrents. Movement gradually ceases and below is a sea of heads. A roar swells up in the distance, as of water falling over a precipice. From the balcony we perceive a dark object, cleaving its way through the mass. The shouting is deafening and the crowd boils up around a carriage drawn by two pairs of tall grey horses, with a magnificent coachman holding the reins and two Cossacks in crimson uniforms towering at the back. Inside the carriage something in white—a vision of loveliness; a fair head bows to the right and to the left. The man sitting in the carriage raises his hand in salute. The iron gates of the Anitchkoff Palace opposite swing open and the grey horses, as if swimming in the black mass, come round in a splendid curve. The thin blare of trumpets is heard, calling the guard of honour to attention. Yet a second, the carriage rolls in through the gateway;

the gates swing back and a wave of humanity beats against them, as if to overtake the white vision. This is the memory of the author, as a boy, of the wedding day of the Empress Alexandra. He remembers the comments of the people on the balcony: "A wedding so soon after a funeral will not bring luck!"

The muzzle loaders on the granite walls of the grim fortress of St. Peter and St. Paul had started firing early in the morning. The Dowager Empress Marie woke up with a start and sat up in bed listening to the dull crashes. On another wintry morning, nearly thirty years ago, the same guns had ushered in her own wedding day . . . but it was better not to think of the past, for to-day she would take off her widow's weeds in honour of the marriage of her eldest son, the Emperor Nicholas. The date had been put off as long as possible after the funeral, but this morning was the utmost limit, because the six weeks of the strict Russian Lent would begin in the afternoon, when the Church refuses to perform the sacrament of marriage. Incidentally, this day was her own birthday. How happy she had been always when this day came round, but better not to dwell on these memories! It was the wedding day of her beloved Nicholas and she had promised to get up early to give him his breakfast, dear child! Then it would be necessary to dress for the ceremony. Dear Nicholas, the poor boy, was dazed with happiness. According to custom he had been forbidden to see his bride on the preceding evening and had sat with the Empress Marie until late at night. His own account of the day is as follows:

November 14th, Monday. My wedding day. After coffee with the family, everybody went to dress. I donned the Hussar uniform and at 11 drove with Misha to the Winter Palace. Along the whole route stood troops waiting for Mamma to drive past with Alix. Whilst the latter was being attired in the Malachite room, we all waited in the Arabian drawing room. At 12:10 the procession started for the Big Church, whence I returned a married man. I had for best men: Misha, Georgie, Cyrill and Serge. In the Malachite room we were presented by the family with an enormous silver swan. Having changed her dress Alix took place with me in a carriage drawn by four horses with an outrider and we drove to the Kazan Cathedral. The streets were so full of people that we scarcely could get through. In the courtyard of the Anitchkoff Palace we received the salute of a guard of honour of Uhlans of the Guard. Mamma was waiting in our rooms to present us with the bread and salt. The whole evening we sat writing answers to telegrams. Dined at 8 o'clock and went to bed early because Alix had a headache.

Long before half past eleven, the appointed time of assembly, the guests began to gather in the halls of the Winter Palace. From this palace to that of Anitchkoff, on the Nevsky Prospect, the Imperial residence and a short distance beyond to the palace of the Grand Duke Serge, till this moment the temporary abode of the Imperial bride, crowds of sight-seers began to collect and to squeeze into every available space allowed them by the troops lining the roadway. Along this route of one and a half miles were stationed the picked troops of the Guard regiments. Escorted by squadrons of lancers and hussars the Imperial bride drove to the Winter Palace soon after eleven amid much cheering and retired to the private apartments with the ladies of honour. The Czar, the Dowager Empress, the King of Denmark and the Prince and Princess of Wales also drove from the Anitchkoff Palace about the same time. The vast reception rooms of the Winter Palace, unrivalled in Europe for their size and magnificence, were thronged by a variegated multitude, whose gold lace, jewels and brilliant uniforms under the blaze of electric light were dazzling to the sight. In each hall members of the aristocracy, courtiers and holders of different ranks and titles were marshalled in order by masters of ceremonies on both sides from door to door, with a gangway kept clear down the centre for the wedding procession.

At the entrance to the chapel the Metropolitan and clergy assembled in their gorgeous stoles and copes. In the Hall of the Armourial Bearings, adorned with gold and silver plate, were ranged the ladies of the Russian society in court costumes, with head-dresses of velvet ornamented with pearls and long white veils, also the nobility and officials of the first four classes. In the next Hall of the Field Marshals, with the life-sized portraits of the latter on the walls, and in the Throne Room of Peter the Great, were gathered the municipal corporations and mayors, the representatives of Russian and foreign commerce and the native and foreign press. The British merchant community was represented by the heads of the well known firms of Hubbard, Clarke and Miller. There were also Tartar and Mohammedan merchants, who gave colour to the scene with their long coats of many-hued silk. In the antechamber and Hall of Nicholas I, the latter being the largest in the Palace, were placed the members of the Czar's military staff, the officers attached to the grand dukes and foreign princes and naval and military officers on active service. In the Concert Hall, which comes next, were waiting the highest dignitaries of the Court and the ladies and maids of honour of the empresses and grand duchesses. Beyond the Concert Hall were private apartments including the Malachite Chamber, from which the Imperial procession started at about twelve-thirty. As the great doors were thrown open for its appearance the guns of the fortress were again heard, firing a salute. First came, two by two, scarlet liveried servants and then at least one hundred and fifty gold-laced gentlemen of the chamber, chamberlains and masters of ceremonies of various grades. The Marshal of the Court and several assistants with their gold sticks of office preceded the bridal party.

The Dowager Empress appeared, leaning on the

arm of her father, the King of Denmark. She was dressed in a rich white court dress with a coronet of pearls and diamonds. Next came the young Czar in Red Hussar uniform, leading his bride, who was attired in a costume of silver brocade with an immense train carried by four chamberlains. On her head was a diamond crown, surmounting a wreath of orange blossoms, brought from the Imperial conservatory at Warsaw in Poland. From her shoulders hung in heavy folds a mantle of gold tissue lined with ermine, which was also supported by the dignitaries who carried her train.

The Prince of Wales wore his Russian dragoon uniform and the Princess of Wales was dressed in a magnificent court costume with court feathers and the diamonds presented to her by the ladies of England. The Duke of York was in British naval uniform. The ribbon of the Order of Hesse was worn by the Czar and most of the grand dukes and princes. All the other members of the Imperial family walked in the procession and the officers and ladies in the suites of the foreign royalties. The Russian maids of honour, who continued the cortège, were dressed in white satin with crimson velvet trains and head-dresses to match with white veils. As the bridal procession slowly paced through the great halls to the church, the guards of honour, posted in each hall with drawn sabres, saluted and the throng on either side bowed low. The church not being large enough to hold one-fifth of the three thousand or more persons who were present, only a few could crowd in after the entry of the Imperial party; among them were the Diplomatic Body, which had assembled in the Throne Room of St. George.

The form of marriage in the Russian Church for all alike is of three parts, each of which in earlier times was often performed separately. First comes the betrothal, or placing and exchange of rings, then the "matrimonial coronation," which is the actual sacrament of marriage and consists in the holding of gilt or golden crowns adorned with medallion images of our Saviour and the Virgin, and finally the "removal" or "deposition of crowns." The service opened with the usual litany, in which the choir took part and two short prayers. Lighted candles were then placed in the hands of the affianced pair, and a censer was swung by the officiating priest. The engagement rings, previously placed upon the altar, were then brought on a golden plate by the priest, who made the sign of the cross with them before the couple to be wedded, saying first to the bridegroom, "The servant of God, Nicholas, betroths himself to the servant of God, Alexandra." The same formula was used in making the sign of the cross before the bride. The rings were then exchanged three times between the bride and groom. A prayer followed supplicating the blessing of the Almighty on the betrothed, after which was intoned the liturgy for the Imperial family. Then the seventy-seventh Psalm was chanted, the choir singing between each verse. In addition to the questions customary in the English ritual, the priest asked the bride and groom each separately: "Have you ever promised yourself to another?" Again a litany, followed by long prayers. Two crowns were then brought, with each of which the priest made the sign of the cross. He then handed them to the "best men" to be held over the heads of the bridegroom and bride, while the latter followed him around the small reading desk placed in the centre of the church. The priest joined their hands beneath his stole and led them in this part of the ceremony. The crowns were held over the heads of the Imperial bridal couple by several of the unmarried grand dukes in turn. The concluding part of the service consisted of a short prayer, after which the bridal pair kissed the holy icons and received the congratulations of their families.

The procession back through the halls of the Palace to the private apartments was performed in the same order as that already described with the exception that the Emperor and his bride, now the Empress Alexandra Feodorovna, took the head in front of his mother and the King of Denmark. The Imperial party soon afterwards returned to the Anitchkoff Palace amid the enthusiastic acclamations of the populace. The semi-state carriages of the Dowager Empress and the Czar and Czarina were each drawn by four grey horses with outriders, and two Cossacks rode in front to clear the road. In contrast, perhaps intentional, to the absurd practice which prevailed during the recent funeral processions, the few police interfered in no way with the crowds, which pressed close on the Imperial carriages and cheered the occupants in the wildest state of excitement. On the Nevsky Prospect, where the Emperor and the Empress stopped to kiss the Image of the Mother of God of Kasan, the carriage was several times unable to proceed through the dense masses of people, who waved their caps and handkerchiefs and shouted for the Czar.

With the evidence supplied above, the reader will be able to compose for himself a complete picture of the events of the day. The author remembers yet one characteristic incident. His grandfather had returned from the Palace, where he had witnessed the bridal procession to and from the church. In his gold-laced uniform, surrounded by his family, the old man sat in a high-backed armchair, sipping the traditional Russian glass of tea with lemon and vividly describing the scenes in the palace. He dwelt on the regal beauty of the young Empress: "By far the loveliest bride I have ever seen," said he. Suddenly, looking round the attentive circle with his keen eyes, he added: "Alexandra Feodorovna is the most beautiful woman in Russia to-day but there is something in her eyes which makes a cold shiver run down my spine." The silence that followed was broken by grandfather's gay laugh: "But the Dowager Empress, my dears, is as young and charming as ever. God give many years to our Mother Dear, Marie Feodorovna!"

CHAPTER VII

THE YOUNG WIFE

UTOCRACY is a hard profession to follow; Nicholas was reminded of the fact after his marriage, when he was denied what he would have liked most, a real honeymoon. The affairs of State and the rules of an exacting Court were to be considered. Under the autocratic régime there was no responsible ministry and decisions could not be taken on any important matter without the Emperor's consent, so that Nicholas was not able to have a holiday. Etiquette demanded that he and Alix should exchange visits with the members of the family, entertain the foreign royalties present in the capital and show themselves to the people. In addition there were the telegrams! The whole world had sent its congratulations; among the messages were many from crowned heads and relations, which Nicholas and Alix were obliged to attend to personally. The morning of the first day of their married life was devoted to the writing of telegraphic answers, while messages continued to arrive in a stream, which showed signs of abating only on the third day.

The Empress Marie came to visit them for a few

minutes in the morning and after lunch Nicholas
drove with Alix in an open carriage to the fortress to
pray at the tomb of the "dear and unforgettable"
father. The crowds in the streets cheered the newly
married couple, but the people who remembered the
drive of Marie Feodorovna through St. Petersburg on
the day after her wedding, thought that the statuesque
beauty of the Empress Alexandra did not provoke the
unbounded enthusiasm which the human loveliness
of Princess Dagmar had called forth nearly thirty
years before. At tea time the family "elbowed its
way in" with presents for Alix and remained an intolerably long time. For dinner the young pair had
the company of the Grand Duke of Hesse, Ernest,
the brother of Alix, and then were obliged to go to
the station to bid good-bye to him and to other de-
parting royalties. Returning home Nicholas and his
young wife found another batch of congratulatory
messages, with which they wrestled until midnight.
They had had a busy day, which does not fit in with
our idea of a perfect honeymoon. On the next morning the attendants had pity on them and, instead of
waking them at eight o'clock as it had been ordered,
called them an hour later. Nicholas was obliged to
dress in a hurry because ministers were waiting to be
received. The young husband saw his wife "during
the whole morning only for a little hour." After
lunch Nicholas snatched a moment to take Alix for
a drive and then had to go for a walk with his
grandfather, the aged King Christian of Denmark.

The Tragic Bride

The time remaining until dinner was again devoted to the writing of telegrams and in the evening the "whole family arrived to have a look at the wedding presents." A week passed in this exasperating fashion. At last the young couple escaped to the country; going to the palace of Tsarskoe Selo for a real honeymoon—four whole days! "I cannot describe the pleasure of living in peace, without seeing any one—the whole day and night together." The joy of Nicholas is touching, when he is able to put down in his diary that "we lunched alone and dined alone too. . . . " And Alix? Her heart was overflowing. Taking the book away from her husband she wrote in her delicate handwriting:

Ever more and more, stronger and deeper my love and devotion crowned my longing for you. Never can I thank God enough for the treasure He has given me for my very own. To be called yours, Sweety, what happiness can be greater. Never shall I forget this place, already dear to me because of remembrances of '89 and now— our first quiet time together. God bless you, my beloved little husband. I cover your sweet face with kisses.

Never did I believe that there could be such utter happiness in this world, such a feeling of unity between two mortal beings. I LOVE YOU —those three words have my life in them.

No more separations! At last united, bound for life and when this life is ended we meet again in the other world to remain together for all eternity Yours, yours!

82

The Young Wife

Even when transported by love to a sphere above dogmatic considerations, Alix could not forget the principles by which her life was to be governed: her religion, her attachment to the past and her firm attitude towards the future, so clearly established that in the passionate exaltation of the honeymoon she could not free herself of their domination. Yet she was a woman with blood in her veins and able to see the humour of small things. Witness the following sentence—written in Russian, a language which she was learning to speak correctly—"It is not well to grind your teeth during the night: your aunt cannot sleep."

When the young couple returned to St. Petersburg things became easier because the foreign royalties had left with the exception of Aunt Alix (Princess of Wales). But the latter and the Empress Marie, delighting in their mutual company, kept very much to themselves. The family soon understood that the young Empress wanted her husband to herself and did not appreciate calls at all times of the day. The mourning imposed by the death of Alexander III had for result that there were few official functions to attend and there was no entertaining. This gave Nicholas and Alix time to enjoy the company of each other, a thing they were only too glad to do. They continued to live at the Anitchkoff Palace of the Empress Marie, while their apartments at the great Winter Palace were being redecorated and furnished

under their personal supervision. On the eve of
the New Year Nicholas remarks:

It was dreadful to stand in church and to think
of the terrible change which happened this year.
But my faith is in the Almighty and I look forward
fearlessly into the New Year. . . . My loss is irreparable, but God has remarked me with a happiness about which I did not dare to dream even;
He has given me Alix.

So the days and months slipped by in a concentrated
enjoyment of each other. On May 14, 1895, Alix
with her usual precision remarks:

*A half year now that we are married, how in-
tensely happy have you made your wifey, you cannot think. God bless you, my own true beloved
husband—daily purer, stronger, deeper.*

On June third we find that husband and wife go
on a pilgrimage to a pavilion in the park of the Peterhoff Palace (near St. Petersburg, on the shore of
the Finnish gulf) to look at their entwined initials,
a souvenir of boy and girl love, which Nicholas
scratched on a window pane ten years before. A
tie is now between them, the strongest tie which
can exist in marriage. Alix whispers the secret
one day into the ear of Nicholas and since then their
thoughts have always returned to it.

*My sweet, old darling mannykins, wifey loves
you so deeply and strongly: you are my one and
all. A few months still and then . . . oh my*

ALEXANDRA FEODOROVNA AND NICHOLAS II WITH OLGA, THEIR FIRST CHILD, 1896

ALEXANDRA FEODOROVNA AND NICHOLAS II ON THEIR WEDDING DAY, 1894

*angel, what intense happiness . . . ours . . .
our very own . . . what happiness can be
greater; only wifey must try and be as good
and kind as possible, else, another little person might suffer from it . . . a big kiss.*

The whole of Russia knew what was expected and
hoped for an heir. On November third the Empress
Alexandra gave birth to her first child: the Grand
Duchess Olga. The country was disappointed, but
Nicholas in the joy of knowing that his beloved Alix
was out of danger was delighted with the daughter.

A day which I shall never forget and during
which I suffered very, very much. Already at
1 A.M. the pains came preventing dear Alix
from sleeping. She lay all day on the bed in
terrible pain, poor dear. I could not bear looking at her. Mamma arrived about 2 P.M. We
remained all the time near Alix. At the stroke of
nine we breathed freely, when we heard the
squawk of a child. During evening prayers the
daughter given us by God was named Olga.
When the terror was past and the excitement had
ceased the event made me feel as if I were in
Heaven. God be thanked: Alix stood the trial
well and in the evening she was in good spirits.

Alix was disappointed. She had hoped to hold
a man child in her arms to give joy to Nicholas and
to satisfy the nation. But the feeling did not last,
when the baby was laid on her breast. Stealing into
the room Nicholas found his wife dozing with a smile

of contentment with her little daughter held tenderly in her arms.

We have not the impression that in the beginning of her married life the Empress Alexandra cared for politics. She left them to her mother-in-law with whom the Emperor took advice daily, because she had been the confidante of Alexander III and knew his views on people and things. Why should the young wife have worried about stupid political questions when she was the queen of love? In her attachment to family life she deliberately relinquished in favour of the Empress Mother the primacy in the affairs of the Court, because they bored her. As far as she was concerned she attended official ceremonies from a sense of duty and not for enjoyment. Her relations with the members of the Imperial family were also on the cool side. She remembered the condescending attitude of the proud grand duchesses when she was only a poor German princess. She meant to obtain from them in full the respect due to her exalted rank. When the women in a family fall out, then men are drawn into the dispute; it was, therefore, natural for Nicholas to adopt his wife's point of view. The relative of whom she saw most was Xenia, the sister of Nicholas, married in the same year as herself to a cousin—the Grand Duke Alexander Michailovitch. Xenia, too, had a little daughter and the young mothers found in their nurseries a common interest to stimulate friendly relations. But, if Alexander III had already kept the members of his

family at a distance, Nicholas II went further in this
direction and his intercourse with most of them was
of a casual nature deprived of sincerity. A rift was
created, lasting for twenty years. When an attempt
to close it was made during the Revolution, it was
too late.

Society was disgusted with the aloofness of the Empress and with her attitude, which deprived it of the
usual occasions to display the bravery of its dresses
and jewellery. Soon, when the name of the Empress
was mentioned, superstitious people began to whisper:
"Ah yes, she is beautiful, but so cold! She became
a bride at a deathbed and was she not married whilst
workmen were yet busy on the tomb of Alexander III?
This is a bad omen!" Then the name was thrown at
her: *Niemka*—the German. Princess Alix, the granddaughter of Queen Victoria, a German! From the age
of six years she had been brought up in England by
her grandmother, and English was more natural to
her than German; her whole habit of life was English. Poor, shy, tragic bride—they called her *Niemka*
and *Niemka* she remained. She never became popular with the nation, though later she tried hard to dispel the preconceived notions which had been formed
about her. It is doubtful, if, in the first happy years,
she even suspected the existence of the black cloud
of libellous insinuations, she was so wrapped up in
her own happiness. There were such important questions to solve too. The nurse sent from England for
the little daughter proved to be bad tempered and it

was necessary to get rid of her. This difficult problem is specially mentioned in the diary of Nicholas, who seems to have exhibited an angelic patience in all things in which Alix was concerned. His reward was her love.

> *Sweet Nicky mine, no words can express how deeply I love you, more and more every day, deeper, truer. Love sweet, do you believe it, do you feel my heart throb so quickly, and only for you, my husband?*　　　　(March 29, 1895)

Their exquisite relations as lovers did not prevent Nicholas and Alix from having their domestic troubles. It was the wife with her quick temper who provoked them and the things she said were not pleasant. She swiftly repented and flew to the side of her beloved Nicky:

> *Forgive me, sweety mine, for any rough word I said to you. When I have been very tired I have answered you gruffly. Pardon me, lovey dear. I at once regretted it from the depth of my heart. God bless you and give you strength, courage and energy in all your undertakings for the good of our beloved Country. I kiss you, fondly, Wifey.*

Nicholas had been trained from childhood to believe implicitly in the divine origin of autocracy. The mysticism in the nature of Alix made it easy for her to accept whole-heartedly the same view. Husband and wife were convinced that Russia had been confided to the Emperor by God and that government was an inherited duty, which could not be shared with other men. Nicholas derived little pleasure from the possession of power of which he was afraid and which he accepted as an inescapable burden. For he had never been made acquainted even with the elementary principles of democracy, which to him meant only revolution. A predominant characteristic of Alix was the shyness which made her suffer intolerably in the company of people whom she did not know well. These circumstances combined to make the intimacy of family life appear both to husband and wife as Paradise. To live one for the other, to see only a few friends, was the ideal to which they aspired and which they tried to attain in planning their intimate existence.

Impressions stored in the brain come to life suddenly and illuminate the past. The author now remembers having as a boy been taken by a friendly commandant of the Palace, in the absence of the Imperial owners, to see their apartments. The majestic empty halls and the richly furnished chambers in which the official part of their existence unrolled the splendour of its ceremonies amazed the eye, but did not leave anything definite to be remembered. All the more vivid is the recollection about the rooms destined for private occupation. They were few: a library with a desk, which appeared absurdly small in comparison with two tiers of enormous bookcases, which themselves seemed dwarfed by the immensity of the room; a sitting room of the Empress smothered in dust sheets and therefore impersonal, and the bedroom. The latter—a great chamber in the angle of the Palace lighted on two sides by great arched windows—contained two objects which attracted attention: the great double bed of some light wood and the iconostas—the collection of holy images, which filled the wall at one side of the bed from the top nearly to the bottom. In the retrospective illumination of a faithful memory the author sees it all: the great bed, symbolic of a united existence, and the wall covered with the closely set icons, glittering with gold and silver and precious stones, with diminutive lights, hung on chains of precious metal, in front of them.

A boyish curiosity led to the exploration of two small dressing rooms and of a large swimming bath to which access was gained through a door disguised by the panelling. That was all. The great bed and the icons were the centre of an oasis in which private life had taken refuge from the coldness of the ceremonial apartments outside. Nicholas and Alix clung together on their little refuge, hating the idea of the arid solitude by which they were encompassed. This was in the magnificence of the Winter Palace in St. Petersburg. The following is a description by an intimate friend of the Empress [1] of her private apartments in the Palace of Tsarskoe Selo, the Imperial residence in the country a score of miles away from the city.

The bedroom of the Emperor and Empress was a large room with two tall windows, opening on to the

---

[1] Mme. Lili Dehn.

Park. . . . A large double bed made of lightish wood
was near the windows between which stood the Empress's dressing table. At the right of the bed was a
little door in the wall, leading to a tiny dark chapel
lighted by hanging lamps, where the Empress was
wont to pray. The chapel contained a table, a praying
stand on which were a Bible and an icon of Christ.
. . . The furniture in the Imperial Palace was covered with flowered tapestry and the carpet was a plain
coloured soft pile. The Emperor's dressing room
was separated from the bedroom by the corridor, and
on the other side were the Empress's dressing room
and bathroom—but, alas for her rumoured extrava-
gancies and her "odd" fancies! The bathroom was
no luxurious place of silver and marble, but an old
fashioned bath set in a dark recess, and the Empress
with her Victorian love for neatness, insisted that the
bath be hidden during the day under a loose cretonne
cover. . . ."

The Imperial couple with unlimited means at their
disposal could have arranged their life on a scale of
luxury and comfort which is customary among proud
millionaires, but their tastes and needs were of the
simplest and the only thing they really wanted was to
be together, to be left by the world to enjoy the company of each other in perfect seclusion. Nicholas only
followed the example of his father Alexander III, who
also was a family man above all things. But times
were changing rapidly and if autocracy was to be preserved it had to play its part as a live national institution, raised on a plane high above the prosaic existence of private individuals.

CHAPTER VIII

RUSSIA IN THE NINETIES

HE year in which the Empress Alexandra had come to Russia was the thirteenth and last of the reign of Alexander III. Courtiers have given to this Emperor the magnificent name of Creator of Peace—*Mirotworetz*—because, peace loving by nature, he had been spared by fate the necessity of going to war. It would have been nearer the mark to have called him the Anaesthetist, for he made it his business to reduce the realm to a state of spiritual slumber. Alexander III had lived through the turmoil of the reforms of the preceding reign which had culminated in the assassination of his father, Alexander II, the Liberator. This threw him into the arms of reaction in its most stupid form.

Autocracy, as we have said, is a hard profession to follow. It demands a combination of three essential qualities: conviction, will and ability. The autocrat must be convinced of his right to govern, he must have the will to impose obedience and he must possess the ability of a statesman, for he is the source of all power in the State. If he doubts the validity of his right to rule he cannot keep his throne. If will is lacking, the autocrat becomes the figurehead for the oligarchic régime of nobles, bureaucrats or soldiers. Lack of statesmanship, on the other hand, makes it useless for him to be convinced of his right, and dangerous to possess will-power, for it will be misdirected.

Alexander III was a sincere autocrat, but his obstinacy, inherited from Hessian ancestors, was a poor substitute for intelligence. Of statesmanlike abilities he possessed less than a fair share. Unable to consolidate autocracy by constructive measures, he tried to preserve it by keeping the nation in a state of mental torpor. Assisted by fanatical reactionaries, by brainless generals and by time-serving officials, Alexander III strove to make Russia a land without politics. The people were asked to surrender their will and conscience into the keeping of the monarch, while to them was generously conceded the privilege of vegetating in animal comfort, so that not a ripple should disturb the placid surface of their spiritual existence. The task of reaction was facilitated by the rot which in the eighties of last century had appeared in the national organism. The generation which in the sixties had co-operated in the liberation of the serfs and in the following reforms no longer existed. After two agitated decades the cooling influence of age had dulled the ardour of the survivors. A new generation, not content with the scope of the reforms, and refusing to wait for their extension by the process of evolution, demanded further liberties, which the Imperial Government was slow to concede. The contrast between Liberal fathers and Radical sons was sharp and the political continuity was interrupted. In his old age, Alexander II, the Liberator, favoured conservative ideas, while the radicals drifted towards anarchistic views. Finding no support in the one and estranged from the others, the Liberals gave up the struggle and ceased to be a power in politics. The field was left to revolutionary groups, which in spite of a restricted membership, professed to represent national aspirations. The situation degenerated into a disgraceful campaign of death by a pack of fanatics against an old man. The supreme tragedy came when Alexander II was blown to pieces by a bomb, for a Liberal constitution was lying on his desk signed and ready to be published on the morrow. The wanton murder was a moral reverse for the Radicals; Russia shrank from them in anger. But the old Liberals were past resurrection and by a natural turn of events the reactionaries obtained the upper hand in the government, and found in Alexander III a willing tool. He decided to ignore the act which his father had just signed and declared for autocracy by divine right. Shocked by the hideous crime and disgusted with extreme views, Russia applauded his resolve and prepared itself to accept the anaesthetic which was mixed for it under the formula: Autocracy, Orthodoxy and Nationality.

In a not too distant future, when the present rulers of the Kremlin will have become a thing of the past, the student of history will inquire into the similarity of their régime with that inaugurated by Alexander III and his advisers. Lenin's cruelty was infinitely greater, but if methods vary, principles remain the same. Lenin, like Alexander III, was for autocratic power, a power exercised "for" the people, but certainly not "through" the people, in fact a dictatorship. Lenin and Alexander III were in agreement on the point that there should be only one religion in the State; for the Emperor this was Orthodoxy, for the Bolshevik apostle—communism. The question of nationality Lenin resolved from the point of view of his narrow doctrine as the exclusive right of the Communist Party to political existence. Alexander III in the same way considered that only the "pure" Russian had the right to full citizenship. Lenin and Alexander III—the bringing together of these two personalities, standing as it seems on opposite poles—is one of the surprising results of a study of Bolshevism not as a unique phenomenon but as a phase in the development of Russian politics. Leaving speculation alone for the present, let us return to the study of precise facts.

The liberation of the serfs in 1861 had been an act of belated justice and in the new Russia, which was called to life, there was a pressing need for the clearing away of the cobwebs of the preceding régime. For this political spring cleaning Alexander II introduced two great reforms: he made the law independent of government and granted autonomy to the provinces. Irremovable judges, united into an independent corporation and assisted by juries, were appointed to administer justice in open court. For the first time in Russian history, the law was free. Fair and equal for all, it promised to become the mainstay of the State as the guardian of civic rights and of legality. In the provinces the people were granted the right of electing councils for the administration of their financial, educational and medical affairs. In the absence of national representation, which had not been created yet, the provincial administrations— *Zemstvos*—became political schools in which the people were prepared for a wider democracy. The *Zemstvos* were the strongholds of liberalism and all over the country the work began of training the masses to a sense of nationhood and political responsibility. The law courts and the *Zemstvos* were the foundation on which a Constitutional State was to be built up by a process of painless evolution.

But autocracy in its very essence is absolute. For it to embark on reforms can mean only voluntary abdication of its "divine" prerogative, or final revolution. Alexander II generously wished to improve the lot of his people and went far to meet the political demands of his time, but he was not prepared to surrender the essential principle of autocracy. The inevitable result was the revolutionary activities of the nihilists. It was a logical necessity for Alexander III, as the active defender of the autocratic principle, to become the declared enemy of the reforms of Alexander II. He could not annul them but he tried hard to cripple them by all means in his power and in every possible way. He directed his attack against the pillars of the democratic régime: the law courts and the *Zemstvos*. No effective opposition could come from public opinion stunned by the tragic end of Alexander II.

The reign of Alexander III was characterized by a vigorous offensive against the independence of the judiciary and the autonomy of the *Zemstvos*. The judges were made once more subject to Imperial caprice and the *Zemstvos* were shorn of their most valued privileges. The cultural work, which had begun so well, was pushed into the background and often stopped. Worst of all: the democratic movement towards national unity was nipped in the bud by the measures intended to keep the peasantry segregated as a class and preserved from the influence of the intellectuals. In its blindness the government thought that it could encourage the peasants to remain faithful to autocracy by the artificial enforcement of obsolete customs of ownership, which made the land the common property of the village community—the *Mir*—which was also collectively responsible for the payment of taxes. This "communism by autocracy" supplied later on the material for the conflagration of the Revolution.

In the scheme of Alexander III the Orthodox Church was an administrative factor. He firmly established the supremacy of Orthodoxy as the religion of the State. But the Church paid a heavy price for this exalted position by losing the remnant of its ancient liberties. When religion becomes an instrument of government there is no time left to attend to things spiritual. The Orthodox clergy, more than ever before, became allied with the administration. In the rural districts, especially, it was often difficult to distinguish between the priest and the policeman. The resulting heavy losses of spiritual prestige became apparent during the Revolution. Concurrently the scope of national education was deliberately reduced. Knowledge was considered to be the source of revolutionary troubles—to be cut down and restricted in every possible way. Autocracy preferred to have an illiterate nation to an educated one with a mind poisoned by the democratic idea.

The supreme folly of the régime was its attitude towards the question of nationality. Peter the Great had welcomed all foreigners. In his day a Scotsman commanded armies, an Italian organized the police, a Swiss advised on foreign affairs and Germans, French, Spaniards and even Arabs served the Empire in serried ranks. No distinction was made so long as Russia profited by the loyal service and superior knowledge of the foreigners. Reigns followed when one nationality or another dropped out of favour. So the French lost their influence during the Revolution of 1793 and the English in the nineteenth century were to a great extent eliminated by the Germans, whose numbers, on the contrary, increased. Alexander II recognized even the right of the Jews to serve the

State and freed them from the disabilities under which they had laboured until then in civil life. But Alexander III changed all this. He wanted to see the "pure" Russian supreme in the State. This meant that to be in favour it became necessary to belong to the Orthodox Church and to assert a Slav origin. The more that descent was open to doubt the more loudly had it to be proclaimed. That Orthodoxy was the touchstone is proved by the fact that Russian sectarians were treated with a harshness, which made their position not much better than that of the Jews.

So much has been said about the part played by the Jews in the Revolution that to discuss this point is opportune. Jewish Revolutionaries have had a great deal to do with the upheaval in Russia, but Lenin, the Apostle, and Bolshevism itself are Russian phenomena. The Revolution was unavoidable, but Jewish men and women assisted its success with their sense of realities and their ruthless executive ability. Here the Czarist régime reaped what it had sown, for the Jewish Revolutionary was its product. In his desire to keep the major part of Russia free from Jewish influence Alexander III crowded the Jews into the Pale —the narrow limits of the Polish provinces—and even there the oppressed people were denied the right of free movement and herded into restricted urban areas. Thrown back into the ghetto, deprived of the right to move, restricted in the right to trade and hedged in by regulations which placed them in the power of the police, the Jews suffered from acute economic and moral distress and the desire for freedom became with them a ruling passion. The Government, although it could herd the Jewish mass into concentration camps, was unable to do without Jewish help altogether. It was easy, swinging the Orthodox censer, to proclaim the triumph of autocracy; but life had to go on and trade and the Liberal professions demanded a live force, a brain power and an executive ability of which there was not enough to go round among the "pure" Russian population. So an exception was grudgingly made in favour of the Jew who was rich or who was clever. The first was not dangerous, but the second developed into a deadly enemy of autocracy. For to the latter was applied the notorious *Numerus Clausus,* that is, the rule of admission by percentage to the enjoyment of the advantages of education. The Jew who was not sufficiently rich to pay a high taxation, could legally escape from the Pale only by producing high educational qualifications. The Government was afraid of Jewish cleverness and had severely restricted the percentage of Jewish children admitted into the public schools, and of Jewish youth allowed to enter the universities. The few lucky candidates were selected by competitive examination. As a result each year only the cleverest children and youths stood a chance of being admitted and this placed them on an intellectual level high above their Christian schoolfellows, who, to be admitted to an educational institution, did not need to worry about percentages. It became a usual thing for Jews to take the gold medals and

EMPRESS ALEXANDRA FEODOROVNA IN PARIS, 1896

other prizes in public schools. In the universities Jewish scholars pressed into the front rank. The result was that in the liberal professions, in finance and in commerce the Jews easily held the first places. As far as brain power was concerned, these were the best of their race in the whole land. Instead of taking steps to absorb these exceptional people in the mass of the nation, the Czarist régime did its best to keep them discontented and apart. It struck at them through their children. The sons and daughters of a Jewish father who by sheer talent had escaped from the grip of the Pale, when they attained majority did not possess automatically the right of remaining outside it. They had to go back unless they produced the same high educational qualifications acquired in deadly competition with other coreligionists. The alternative was: cringing before the authorities, bribing the police, or outwardly complying with the Orthodox faith as a last recourse. So it happened that by the act of the Government itself a group of Jews was created with a brain power above the average and kept up to the mark by unceasing persecution. Proud of its intellectual record achieved under such unfair conditions these people demanded the right to serve the State. This was refused as a general rule or given on rare occasions as an exceptional favour. The above picture explains why many revolutionary leaders were to be found among the Jews. The same remarks apply to other nationalities which supplied their revolutionary quota for the same reason. Next to Lenin, the Russian, we, therefore, find Trotsky, the Jew, Dzershinsky, the Pole, and Stalin, the Georgian.

At the time when Nicholas II became Emperor the land was outwardly enjoying a deep calm. The Little Father of the moujiks, poetically glorified by Russian sycophants and gullibly accepted by Europe, seemed to be supreme. A policed Church, a depraved nobility, a heartless bureaucracy, a muzzled press, served the ends of autocracy. The army was looked upon more as an instrument for suppressing internal enemies than for national defence. And supreme above all and penetrating all was the police; that is, the organization which by lip service to the autocratic ideal had been able to substitute itself for the law and which had prostituted the will and the conscience of the people. The position of the Government was rendered stronger by the excellent state of its finances, which through the efforts of a remarkable minister, Witte, had been improved beyond recognition. The reserve of gold accumulated by him in the vaults of the Imperial State Bank supplied the régime with its strongest weapon and at the same time with an excellent argument against the attacks of foreign detractors of the autocratic principle. Outwardly, therefore, when Nicholas came to the throne, all was calm. But under the placid surface the revolutionary ferment continued its work. When in the first days of his reign Nicholas received various delegations, there was one among these—the delegation of a *Zemstvos*—which had the courage to speak about the need of democratic reforms. The Emperor told them to forget these "impossible" dreams. He would have done better to have listened to the warning voices. But he sincerely believed that his father had been right and that autocracy was the best—the only form of government suitable for Russia. He also believed in his divine right and Alix, his beloved wife, believed in this right even more than he did himself.

CHAPTER IX

THE PACT WITH HEAVEN

THE letters, written by the Empress Alexandra to her husband during the Great War, when he was away at the front and she was busy controlling the activities of ministers, refer often to the democratic reforms which the nation demanded with growing insistence. The attitude of Alexandra is irreducibly hostile, for she believes in the sanctity of autocracy: it is from God! To stiffen the resistance of Nicholas she reminds him that at the coronation he had sworn to maintain autocracy and that it is his duty to transmit it intact to his son.

The question of the Czar's oath at the coronation is a difficult one to answer, because the service of the ceremony does not contain any words of the nature described by the Empress. What she, probably, has in mind is the ancient prayer, the only one which Czars at their coronation recited aloud, and kneeling:

Oh Lord, God of our Fathers, King of Kings, Thou, who by Thy Word hast created Everything, and in Thy Wisdom hast set Man to govern the World in Righteousness and Justice. Thou hast chosen me as Czar and Judge of Thy People.

The Pact with Heaven

I confess Thy unfathomable Solicitude for me and rendering Thanks, I bow before Thy Majesty. And Thou, my Lord and Master, make me skilled in the Task, which Thou hast set me; teach me, and guide me in this great Service.

Grant me Wisdom worthy of Thy Throne; let it descend from the Holy Heavens, so that I know what is agreeable in Thy Sight, and what is just according to Thy Will?

Let my Heart be in Thy Hand, to fulfil All that is most expedient for the People entrusted to me, and to Thy Glory.

So on the Day, when Thou sittest in Judgment, I too shall be able to render Account without Shame: through the Grace and Mercy of Thine only Son—with Him may'st Thou be blest, together with Thine All-Holy and Good and Lifegiving Spirit in all Eternity! Amen.

In this prayer the climax of the religious function is attained. After it the clergy and the congregation kneel, while the Czar stands erect in the glory of the crown, and Imperial vestments. The eldest metropolitan pronounces a prayer of thanksgiving and the ceremony proper of the coronation is considered to have been performed.

The Empress has, no doubt, this moment of high tension in mind, when she speaks so definitely about the Czar's oath. A mystically inclined mind, like hers, reads into the words of the ancient prayer a pact with the Almighty—a pact between God and the man chosen to be Czar and judge over His people. Guidance must come from God; there can be no intermediary between the Czar and the people, except God! This is the Russian formula of autocratic power; the people are the flock, entrusted to the Imperial shepherd by his Lord and Master. While Nicholas pronounced the words in the hushed church, Alexandra listened, repeating them after him in her heart as a solemn dedication of the realm to the service of God. In the precise way, which was hers, she had the service explained to her beforehand; she was penetrated with the importance of the moment. Later, during the ceremony, she saw her husband anointed with the holy oils and then entering the closed altar to partake of holy communion—the only layman in Russia so privileged —under both forms as the clerics. Alexandra knew then that Nicholas was, indeed, a man apart, covered with the mantle of a heavenly protection: the autocrat of all the Russias. This pact with heaven became the creed of the Imperial pair. They resisted attempts to reduce by democratic measures the power given by God. When obliged to make concessions, they did all they could to curtail them at the earliest opportunity as contrary to the will of God and they resisted suggestions of reforms until it was too late and their tragic fate could not be averted any longer.

It is important to note that the idea of the pact of autocracy with heaven was not invented by the Empress Alexandra. When Alexander I, a great-grand-uncle of Nicholas II, who reigned in the beginning of the nineteenth century, showed a velleity to introduce democratic reforms, Karamzine, the famous historian, presented a memorandum in which he developed the idea that autocracy is of a godly origin and that the sovereign has a compact with heaven to maintain intact the autocratic power. The object of Karamzine was to prove that autocracy is not as much a privilege as a holy duty.

While in May, 1896, in the ancient Kremlin, the coronation ceremonies of Nicholas and Alexandra unrolled their splendour according to an antique ceremonial which we have described elsewhere [1] the scene was being set for the tragedy, which in the eyes of the nation was destined to stamp the occasion as one for mourning rather than for joy. The superstitious Russians saw in it the proof of the bad luck which Alexandra was suspected from the first of bringing to the nation. For the popular feast on the plain of the Khodinka was to take place two days later and workmen were giving the last lookover to its preparations, made on a lavish scale.

The wish of Nicholas had been that the programme of the festivities of his own coronation should follow in every detail that of his father. The Minister of the Court had provided, therefore, for the amusement of two hundred thousand citizens of Moscow and peasants from the surrounding villages. This was the number which had been catered for in 1883 at the coronation of Alexander III. But the multitude which came streaming from all parts for the feast was much

---

[1] V. Poliakoff, *Mother Dear: The Empress Marie of Russia and Her Times.*

greater; it is estimated that by five o'clock in the morning there were about half a million people converging on to the plain so as not to miss the fun.

The Khodinka is a wide plain near Moscow. Military reviews, race meetings and popular entertainments are held there several times in the year. For the coronation feast the plain had been prepared as if for a country fair. Scattered over it were bandstands, open air theatres, roundabouts, greasy poles and platforms for acrobats and other performers. The chief attraction was the "Czar's Gift," provided for each guest: a tin cup, enamelled and decorated with the initials of the Emperor and the double-headed eagle, a piece of gingerbread and a packet of sweets, the whole contained in a large red and yellow cotton handkerchief, imprinted with a view of the Kremlin. To assuage the thirst of the multitude there was a formidable array of barrels with beer and mead. At one side of the plain were the stands, for the Court and society to look down upon the sea of humanity. In the centre of the stands was the Imperial pavilion, on the high balcony of which the Emperor and his consort would come out in the afternoon to show themselves to the people and to admire the procession of decorated cars and gigantic figures, which at that time would traverse the plain. But the organizers of the feast had made a fatal mistake.

On previous occasions the "Czar's Gift" had been distributed to the people at various points of the large plain and congestion at the entrances was thus

avoided. On the present occasion the officials decided
to improve upon this plan. Solid barricades were
established at the entrances, which led through nar-
rowing passages to turnstiles, where the populace
would receive the gifts across special counters. The
scheme looked well on paper, but the authorities had
not foreseen the unprecedented invasion by the immense multitude. The few police and troops present
at that early hour were impotent to arrest and to
break up the movement of the human mass towards
the entrances. Confusion started in the moment the
people began to be admitted; the men behind the
counters increased it by taking fright and beginning
to throw the parcels into the crowd, so as to get rid
of them. The human torrent, with the momentum
of an ever growing mass at the back, burst through
the turnstiles, destroying them and pushing in the
counters and solid walls of the booths at the entrances.
In their criminal negligence the organizers had omit-
ted to fill in a sandpit, which in the form of a trench
about fifteen feet deep and twice as broad lay at the
back of the entrances and across the way on to the
plain itself. They had thrown a few light wooden
bridges over it. The mass of humanity, bursting
through the entrances, was carried by pressure from
behind straight towards the trench, the bridges over
which broke down in a moment. Hundreds, thousands
were pushed to the brink. They fought madly to
save themselves, but the torrent pressed on from behind and they were thrown down by those who stood

behind them, and who in the next second themselves
became the victims of the irresistible movement.
Those who fell were trampled to death by countless
feet; those who were crushed in the mass could not
fall and inanimate bodies remained upright, wedged
in among frenzied humanity. A wail of anguish arose
from the crunching turmoil, while multitudes continued to pour in. Every ridge, every hole in the
ground had its separate tragedy embedded in the general catastrophe. Groups of people and single individuals managed to escape and came staggering out
through the narrow passage between the trench and
the barricades. Their garments were torn off their
backs and the eyes in their disfigured faces were those
of madmen. The chaos lasted for nearly two hours
before the police, the firemen and the troops, which
had been rushed up, managed to arrest the pressure
from behind and begin the work of rescue. The
trench was a sickening sight: it was full of bodies.
Those who lay below had had the life crushed out
of them and those who escaped death were terribly
maimed. All over the ground bodies lay with disfigured faces, broken ribs and some of them reduced
to pulp, as if by a gigantic pestle. Trucks were rushed
up to carry the wounded to the hospitals and to cart
away the dead. The exact number of victims has never
been made known. The wounded and maimed treated
in the hospitals of Moscow were one thousand one
hundred and thirty-eight and from the trench alone
more than a thousand bodies were taken. The dead

Copyright, 1896, by the Illustrated London News   THE CORONATION OF THE CZAR

were found in out-of-the-way places, for people had staggered away only to collapse in the free air. A tragic find was that of more than thirty bodies in a disused well. The boards over the mouth had given way under the weight of the crowd. Wedged in under the corpses were two live beings—raving madmen. While truck after truck rolled away with its load of suffering or dead hidden precariously under tarpaulins, the people continued to arrive on the plain in endless torrents, this time carefully canalized from afar by bodies of troops. By midday there were hundreds of thousands packed on the Khodinka, most of whom ignored the happenings of the morning. Ticketholders for the stands, as they drove up in their carriages, met on the way the trucks with their grisly load. There had been little time, and many bodies which could not be taken away were carried aside and covered with greenery and bunting to hide them from the eyes of the public. When the Emperor stepped on the balcony of his pavilion and bowed to the people, corpses were hidden not more than a hundred yards away from him. Those near Nicholas saw that he was deadly pale and deeply moved, but the immense crowd which acclaimed him from the plain could not see this or that the Empress by his side was tearing her lace handkerchief to pieces in a nervous effort to refrain from breaking down. So the legend was born of the callousness of Nicholas and of Alexandra. We may be certain that they did not know the extent of the catastrophe. The authorities did all in their power to hide it from them, so as to shield Grand Duke Serge, who, as Governor General of Moscow, was the person responsible for the safety of its population. Unfortunately the inquiry into the Khodinka catastrophe was conducted so as to cover the high-placed culprits; only underlings were punished. On the evening of the same day the Emperor and Empress attended the splendid ball given in their honour by the Count of Montebello, the French Ambassador. The atmosphere was one of deep gloom. But Moscovites standing below the brilliantly lighted windows grumbled: "the *Niemka* dances, what does she care: she is accustomed to funerals!" This illustrates the danger of the cast-iron rules of an inhuman etiquette, which exposes its victims to being accused of insensibility to the sufferings of ordinary mortals. We remember reading in the diary of Nicholas the mention of a band playing during lunch, while Extreme Unction was being administered to his dying father. The son was shocked but did nothing.

With what delight Nicholas and Alix, after the pomp of the coronation, returned to the comparative simplicity of their life at Tsarskoe Selo! Their private apartments were an enchanted castle to which they withdrew to escape from the horde of courtiers and officials in the Palace. A few trusted body servants were permitted to enter the sanctuary, but even the dressers of the Empress were forbidden to appear in her bedroom before she herself had attended to her toilet and put on a morning gown. The Mauve Room, so called because the scheme of its decorations was in this favourite colour, was the bower to which Nicholas escaped from his study, where he received ministers and generals and laboriously worked through mountains of State papers. Husband and wife sat together, reading, writing letters and, especially, talking, for Alix was told all that was in the mind of Nicholas. Their baby girl was brought in by her English nurse and there was cooing and talking in the universal baby language. Walks and drives were taken in the fine parks, which surround the Imperial residence,

CHAPTER X

A VISIT TO EUROPE

HE peaceful existence, which Nicholas and Alix loved, was interrupted by their departure for a series of State visits to foreign countries. Etiquette demanded that the Emperor should return the courtesy paid to him by other sovereigns who had attended his coronation themselves or through deputies. Above all it was necessary for him to show himself in Paris, because the famous Franco-Russian Entente was to be consolidated. This alliance had been the outstanding event in foreign politics during the reign of Alexander III, who had overcome his prejudice against the republican form of government, because of the fear inspired in him by Germany's alliance with Austro-Hungary and Italy.

The Empress, who at the time was in a state which the precious language of court circulars described as "peculiarly delicate," insisted on accompanying the Emperor and, naturally, the baby—their eldest daughter, the Grand Duchess Olga—could not be left behind. As the gauge of the Russian railways is broader than that of those of Western Europe, a special Imperial train had been built, replica of the one used inside the country, so that the travellers wherever they went could use their own saloons and sleeping cars arranged to suit their taste. For the sea voyage an old friend, the *Polar Star,* was available and in Copenhagen the *Standard,* a new yacht, specially designed for the use of the Imperial family, had just been completed.

Before going abroad the Emperor with the Empress travelled to Nijni-Novgorod, an old city on the great Russian river, the Volga, where an Industrial and Art Exhibition had been organized. The visit is of historical interest, because the ancient bodyguard of the Czars, the *Ryndy* was reconstituted for this occasion from the sons of the wealthiest merchants of Moscow. Their uniform—a copy of the original one —consisted of a long white cloth coat, bordered with ermine, with an extremely high collar, trimmed with gold lace and lined with red silk, white *safian* boots and a tall stiff cap of white cloth, trimmed with ermine and a jewelled aigrette. The coat, open in front, showed a silk shirt of a dark brown colour. The *Ryndy* was armed with gleaming battle-axes of silver and wore necklaces of precious stones. This Slavophil attempt to renew the splendour of the past was made ridiculous by the fact that, when the Emperor asked one of the brilliant youths for his name, he received the answer: "Mayer, your Majesty!" for among the merchants in Russia there was a strong German element.

The first State visit was to Vienna, to the oldest of the monarchs of Europe, the Emperor Francis, who in honour of his guests deployed all the pomp and splendour of the ancient Austrian ceremonial. Nicholas was accompanied by the Prince Lobanoff, Minister for Foreign Affairs, who profited by the occasion to discuss with Count Goluchowsky, his Austrian colleague, the situation in Turkey, which was just passing through one of its innumerable crises. After several days of ceremonies and banqueting at Vienna, Nicholas with his wife returned to Russia for the consecration of a cathedral at Kieff. Crossing the frontier back into Russia Nicholas had the train stopped in a particularly beautiful spot. This holding up of trains, often for several hours, was an Imperial privilege, which was exercised irrespective of the resulting dislocation of ordinary traffic. Nicholas and Alix got out to take a walk and Prince Lobanoff was sent for, as the Emperor desired to discuss with him the results of the Vienna conversations. No sooner had the Minister descended than he was taken ill and in a moment he died from cerebral hæmorrhage, without having had the time to acquaint his master with the decisions reached with Count Goluchowsky. The impression of this sad incident was dissipated by the arrival in Kieff, where a splendid reception had been prepared by the authorities and by the municipality.

Kieff, the ancient capital, which was a city when Moscow was a forest and St. Petersburg a swamp, is situated on the high bank of the broad Dnieper. Its churches are the most ancient in Russia and the

A Visit to Europe

Petcherskaya Lavra—a monastery—with its mysterious caves and underground passages, in which lie mummified bodies of saints and martyrs, is an object of national veneration, to which thousands of pilgrims come to obtain remission of their sins and a promise of Paradise. In olden days Kieff was the seat of that Grand Duke Vladimir, who in his youth was a pagan, but, having taken for wife the sister of two Byzantine emperors, he allowed himself to be converted and then baptized his people by driving them into the Dnieper. During four preceding reigns a cathedral had been in process of erection as a monument to St. Vladimir. It was to be inaugurated in the presence of the young Emperor and of his lovely Empress as a worthy continuation of the coronation ceremony in Moscow. Also, in one of the city squares a bronze statue of Nicholas I, the great-grandfather of the Emperor, was to be unveiled.

With a devout interest Alix took part in a great religious festival of the Orthodox Church. She was deeply moved and attracted by the experience. The consecration of the cathedral proceeded according to an ancient complicated ceremonial. The Emperor and Empress walked behind the clergy, arrayed in gorgeous vestments and copes. The procession, reverently bearing holy icons and holding aloft sacred banners, moved round the building inside and out, while powerful choirs chanted psalms and blue clouds of incense arose in the still air from rhythmically swung censers. A visit to the *Petcherskaya Lavra* followed where the Imperial pair piously kissed the saintly relics. It was unfortunate that the festivities were saddened by the news that a pleasure steamer had capsized on the Dnieper taking nearly two hundred people to a watery grave. But already the Imperial train was carrying Nicholas and Alix away from Kieff towards the Silesian frontier, not far from which, in the industrial town of Breslau, William II was awaiting them at the head of an imposing array of troops.

The German Emperor's intention was to capture the friendship of the young Emperor. Alexander III had treated his German colleague coolly and this was ascribed to the influence of his Danish wife, the Empress Marie Feodorovna. William considered that he had a claim on the gratitude of Alix for having backed her marriage with Nicholas. Also he expected her to remember that she was a German princess. But Alix preferred to think of herself as the granddaughter of the Queen of Great Britain; moreover by education and sympathy she was quite English. She resented the patronizing airs of the German Emperor and treated him with a distinct coldness. As for Nicholas, he had inherited his father's instinctive dislike for William II, which friendly overtures on the part of the latter could make him forget only for short periods. The toast pronounced by William II at the State banquet at Breslau was full of gushing sentiment. Nicholas' answer was cold and formal. Not to be deterred William II offered his yacht to take his Imperial guests from Kiel to Denmark; the offer was politely declined under the pretext that the *Polar Star* was lying there all ready for the trip.

At Kiel a visit was paid to Prince Henry of Prussia, Great Admiral of the German fleet and brother of William II. His wife was Irene, an elder sister of the Empress. The travellers then embarked on the *Polar Star* for Copenhagen, where they were met by the Dowager Empress, Marie Feodorovna, who with her younger children, Grand Duke Michael [1] and Grand Duchess Olga,[2] had been staying with her aged parents at the Castle of Bernstorff. Nicholas was proud to show his beautiful wife to the Danish relations. After staying a few days at Bernstorff Nicholas and Alix paid a visit to the King of Greece at his villa at Smidstrup.[3] But Queen Victoria was waiting impatiently to welcome her granddaughter and the Imperial party embarked in the new *Standard,* which, convoyed by the *Polar Star,* proceeded across the North Sea towards Leith, the port of Edinburgh. This was the Empress's first trip in the yacht which in the following year was to become her floating home in summer. Later, when the War put an end to cruising, she always remembered the *Standard* with longing regret.

---

[1] Murdered by the Bolsheviks in 1918.

[2] Married to Prince Peter of Oldenburg (Russian Line), whom she divorced, and married in 1916 Colonel Kulikowsky. Now living in Denmark.

[3] This was William, a brother of Marie Feodorovna, who had become George, King of Greece in 1863. He was married to Grand Duchess Olga Constantinova, an aunt of Nicholas II. He was murdered at Salonika in 1913.

The Tragic Bride

Queen Victoria was in the sixtieth year of her prosperous reign and Great Britain and the Empire were making preparations to celebrate the event with due solemnity. The arrival of the Queen's favourite granddaughter, who by becoming the wife of a powerful Emperor had added lustre to the name of the sovereign, received, therefore, particular attention from the public. The Government, anxious to conciliate the young Emperor, fell in readily with the wish of the Queen that he and his wife should be given an imposing reception. The Channel Squadron assembled in the Firth of Forth to salute the Imperial yacht as she approached Leith. The Prince of Wales, accompanied by Lord Salisbury, the Prime Minister, and by the Russian Ambassador, put off in a steamer to welcome the Emperor and Empress and to bring them into Leith harbour. At the dockside was a gathering of distinguished people and addresses were presented by the civic authorities of Leith and Edinburgh. The guns of the Castle thundered a salute as the Emperor and Empress with the Prince of Wales drove in an open carriage with four horses and postilions to the station, where a special train had been prepared to take them north to Ballater, in the Highlands, from where a carriage road leads to the royal castle of Balmoral.

Precautions had been taken to guard against any attempt to wreck the train. A light pilot engine ran in front; a detachment of British police and Russian detectives travelled on the train itself and the line was patrolled by agents of the railway company and local constables. These measures were not unnecessary, because Scotland Yard had been able to expose a plot for dynamiting the Emperor. Warned from America, British police officers, after clever work in Belgium and France, had discovered near Antwerp a fully equipped laboratory for the production of bombs. Several men were arrested as accomplices, the principal among them being F. Tynan, a well known Fenian, believed to have been fourteen years before the mysterious Number One, the chief of the "Invincible" plot, which led to the assassination of Lord Frederick Hamilton and Mr. Burke in the Phœnix Park in Dublin. The precautions taken to guard the person of the Russian sovereign never failed to excite the curiosity of the public. People spoke with bated breath about mysterious anarchists and deadly plots, often without the slightest foundation in fact.

Granny had arranged a Highland welcome for her dear Alix. At the station, at Ballater, a company of the historic Black Watch formed the guard of honour and the no less famous Scots Greys, of which Nicholas had been appointed honorary colonel, furnished the escort for the open carriage, drawn by four grey horses, in which the Imperial guests left for Balmoral. The Queen's pipers met her guests with a shrill *pibroch* of welcome and then played the procession to the castle. As it was already dark the Balmoral Highlanders marched in serried ranks at the sides of the procession, carrying resinous torches, while bonfires were alight at frequent intervals along the route. The aged Queen, to do honour to the Emperor and Empress, came out on to the porch to meet them. She welcomed Alix with emotion and bade Nicholas cordially welcome. The visit to Balmoral lasted a week, during which Nicholas was given the opportunity to shoot over the neighbouring grouse moors and to do some deer stalking, while the Queen and Alix undertook drives during which favourite views were visited and admired. When the Russian sovereigns, after having planted two trees of remembrance, left Balmoral for Portsmouth, the same honours were rendered to them as at their arrival. In comparison with the comfort of modern travelling it is amusing to note that the special train in which they travelled from Scotland was not supplied with a dining car and stops were made, one at Preston and another at Oxford, to give the travellers an opportunity to partake of breakfast and of lunch at the railway buffets.

At Portsmouth there was an assembly of naval and military officers in full uniform to salute the Emperor. As the Imperial party went on board their yacht, the *Polar Star,* a salute from the guns of the Channel Squadron thundered forth. The Imperial yacht glided out into the Channel, accompanied by the British ships. Midway across a French fleet was met, which took over the duties of an escort. The sea was very rough, but Nicholas and his wife came out on the bridge to see the British warships in impeccable order turn away homewards, while the French closed in to take their places: a portent of the coming Anglo-Franco-Russian Alliance.

The British public had exhibited a lively interest in the Imperial visit and was delighted to admire in the Russian Empress the Princess Alix, well known to it as the granddaughter of the Queen and the daughter of the "lamented Princess Alice." Society, however, which at that time was the prey of a strict Victorian etiquette, viewed with reproof a certain levity in the Empress's choice of dress. Not without amusement we read in the respectable *Graphic* a stiff comment:

Charming and graceful as the Russian Empress is, it is to be hoped that she is not going to set the fashion for us—that of travelling in such fine clothes as Her Imperial Majesty affects. She alighted from one sea voyage in a pale blue dress, fawn mantle trimmed with white ostrich feather collar and a bonnet of white and blue. Another long railway voyage was set forth upon in a light pink silk gown and a delicate heliotrope mantle and white bonnet. Going on the same journey, the Duchess of Connaught wore "a real English costume"—a dark brown tweed tailor-made dress and coat.

This fine dress, unsuitable in view of the sooty travelling to which the British public was obliged to submit, seems to have made a considerable impression, for the staid *Times* also commented at length upon the "pink silk dress with train, heliotrope coloured travelling cloak and cape with white lace, trimmed with white fur at the throat, small bonnet to match cape, decorated with heliotrope, white and light blue coloured flowers."

The visit to France was intended to be and was a demonstration to the world of the friendship uniting the two countries. The French Government and people did their utmost to greet Nicholas as their friend and ally. From the moment the sovereigns stepped on shore at Cherbourg they were surrounded with a hospitality the warmth of which overstepped the limits of the official programme. Nicholas obtained from the Parisians ovations which he could never have expected in his own country. The French showed in every possible way their exuberant joy at having among them the Russian Emperor, whose father had promised to stand by France against the overwhelming might of Germany. The visit was also a personal triumph for the Empress. She took the hearts of the Parisians by storm not by what she said—she was generally silent—but by her exquisite loveliness. She was then at the height of her beauty and motherhood had added a soft roundness to her face, which made it enchanting. Satisfaction at the success of the visit, at the success of her beloved husband, made her look kindly at the world, filling her eyes with light. She passed through the ceremonies as the Queen of Beauty. The most charming ceremony of all was the opening of the new bridge, which in one flat arch boldly spans the Seine and is known the whole world over as the bridge of Alexander III. The Empress, all in white, was a lovely vision. A group of white-robed girls approached, bearing among them a beautiful silver-wrought vase—a gift from Paris to its guests; the Empress made a step forward to receive it, and those who saw the picture she presented at that moment never forgot it.

Before leaving France the Imperial couple went from Paris to Châlons, where, on the field made famous by the victory of Roman Gaul over the Huns, the French Army deployed seventy thousand men to do honour to the Russian monarch. A visit was paid also to the venerable Cathedral of Rheims, where more than eight hundred years before a Russian Princess, Anne, the daughter of the Grand Duke of Kieff-Yaroslaff, had been married to King Henry I of France. The manuscript of the Gospels in the Slavonic language, which she brought in her dowry, still exists.

CHAPTER XI

THE TRAGIC CHANGE

N the span of a lifetime, character changes considerably. Here is the difficulty of the conscientious biographer: he may not restrict himself to the painting of a portrait; it is rather his duty to present impressions of personality, by which the reader may visualize the hero or heroine at various moments of the story. If we know only the shy and lovely Alix—the woman at the hearth—with whom we have already made ourselves acquainted, we shall not be able to understand the haughty Alexandra—the autocratic Empress—of the period of the Great War. Of her we possess a character portrait painted by herself. It is to be found in the letters which she wrote to her husband. The Revolution has thrown these intimate documents into the world, and the soul of the woman stands naked before us. The salient feature is a tremendous willpower. Alexandra's words are the words of love, but the will to conquer is concealed behind them. Claiming the rights of a loving wife and of a devoted counsellor Alexandra installs herself as mistress in the mind of Nicholas, whose weak resistance is easily overcome.

The Tragic Change

In the nature of Alexandra the harmony between the constituting elements has been destroyed. Will-power leads into a blind alley because the capacity to weigh the intrinsic value of things is lacking. Alexandra wants to be a good woman and to make the whole world good. But her goodness is like a room the walls of which are embellished with maxims, beautifully embossed on pieces of cardboard. It is letter perfect, but we miss the human touch. There is no spontaneity about it, and so mechanically is it organized that the refreshing possibility of a mistake is ruled out. Alexandra knows exactly what is good in the world and what is evil. The quality of mercy is foreign to her. She feels no pity, and has little sympathy for people when they fall short of her ideal. She affects an attitude of Christian humility, which permits her to speak complacently of her own virtues.

The haughty coldness of Alexandra, and a congenital disability to understand another person's point of view, make the world empty around her. Yet in her proud heart lingers a desire to find human sympathy. She wants to be loved. But her efforts to obtain popularity are clumsy and casual. She wants to have friends who love her for herself and not for her rank. As she has repulsed the advances of her family and has erected a barrier between herself and society, she is obliged to give her friendship to people whose presence near her surprises us.

Alexandra's fund of knowledge is poor. She knows little about the country of which her husband is the ruler, and she has not met its people. Their history is for her a closed book and she ignores their present condition. Her political judgment proves that she is not acquainted with current events or with the essential elements of the international situation. She knows odds and ends of things, like her quotations of poetry, mostly on sentimental subjects. She is a good wife and mother. Her interest in the welfare of her husband and her children is touching and sustained. She looks after their physical comfort and enters into the smallest details. But in all that Alexandra undertakes we detect the presence of a morbid feeling of self-centred interest. She watches her health carefully, for often she is unwell. She suffers from a nervous irritation depressing to herself and disagreeable for all those who come near her.

Alexandra's letters of the War period show her to us as a strong-willed woman with a theoretical goodness, neutralized by a cold temperament; a woman with a strong sense of duty towards her husband and children, but with her mental balance upset by neurasthenia. There are thousands of women like this in the world. But Alexandra is the wife of the Emperor. She is also an ardent mystic. In the last fateful years of the existence of the dynasty, her strong will makes her the mistress over the weak mind of her husband. She is the real ruler of the State, and her action is governed by the fact that she worships at the mystic shrine.

Deprived at an early age of her mother and brought

up under conditions which cramped her soul and soured her disposition, the sweet child, who had been called Sunny, began to show a shrewish disposition. Love, enfolding her in its fragrant embrace, made her look at life with a kinder eye. Alix developed into a warm-hearted woman, prevented only by her shyness from endearing herself to the world. Upon Nicholas she showered the treasures of a beautiful affection. In politics she was ready to bow to his superior knowledge. But after twenty years, if the characterization of her given above is true, she was much changed. Things must have happened to alter her, bringing out the least sympathetic traits of her nature. Step by step we must trace the tragic sequence of events which transformed the tender Alix into an autocratic Empress.

In the month of June of 1899 a daughter was born to Nicholas and Alix. This child, Marie, was a disappointment to her parents: she was the third girl in the family [1] and they had hoped for a son to be the heir to the throne. A few weeks later the Grand Duke George, brother of Nicholas and heir apparent died in the Caucasus under tragic circumstances. For years he had been a hopeless consumptive and the end did not come as a surprise. As the Emperor had no man child, his youngest brother, Michael, became heir apparent.

In November of the same year, during a stay of the family at their castle in the Crimea, Nicholas fell

---

[1] The second daughter Tatyana was born in 1897.

ill. Like his father he disliked doctors, and only when the condition became grave was a specialist sent for. He diagnosed the case as typhoid fever. The principal ministers and the elder grand dukes met to discuss a situation rendered delicate by the fact that the Empress was known to be with child. But the law of succession was clear: if Nicholas died, Michael had to be proclaimed Emperor. If the posthumous child turned out to be a boy the new sovereign could abdicate in his favour. All were certain that Michael would not hesitate to do so, but all agreed that the throne could not be left vacant for a single moment. It so happened that from that day the illness of Nicholas took a turn for the better and the discussion which had taken place was forgotten by the participants. But the Empress had come to know of the decision taken and considered it a deliberate attempt to deprive her unborn child of the Crown. In the summer of the following year her hopes of having a son were again disappointed: a fourth daughter, Anastasia, was born to her. The desire to have an heir became an obsession. In this way the ground was prepared for the appearance of the notorious charlatan, "Doctor" Philippe of Lyons.

It is said of Philippe that he began life as a butcher. But, whatever his original profession, he found that the income derived from it was not sufficient for his needs. He supplemented it by giving "spiritual" treatment to credulous people. That he possessed some hypnotic powers and a clever brain there is no doubt.

The Tragic Change

Money began to come in and the "doctor's" fame spread beyond Lyons. People with nervous diseases and people who imagined themselves to be so afflicted, came to the healer and many became his steadfast adherents. Among these were the two Russian grand duchesses: Stana and Militza, known at Court and in society as the Black Women, for they were the daughters of Nicholas, King of Montenegro. The Empress Marie Feodorovna, wife of Alexander III, had had the girls educated in Russia and then married them off to members of the Imperial family.[2] These ladies were at that time in the good graces of Alexandra, whom they had charmed by a respectful attitude which the other ladies of the family refused to adopt. So when at their invitation Philippe came to Russia, it was easy for them to persuade the Empress to take an interest in the "healer."

By hypnotic tricks and clever patter Philippe convinced the Empress, and also the Emperor, of his superhuman power. To the disgust of the Empress-Mother, Philippe became a constant caller at Court, where he arranged spiritual séances for his august clients. Alexandra believed that Philippe would be able to foretell the time when she would have a son. Philippe became a "friend" and then "our friend," who in his universal wisdom was expected to advise

---

[2] Stana married a Duke of Leuchtenberg (of the Russian Line), whom she later divorced to become the wife of Grand Duke Nicholas Nicolayevitch, the Commander-in-Chief in the Great War. Militza married the Grand Duke Peter, a brother of the second husband of Stana.

on many matters, even those which had no connexion with his alleged science. As Philippe was often at Court it was decided that he must have a fitting rank; he was appointed an Actual Counsellor of State. What he himself wanted was an official acknowledgment of his medical standing. To satisfy his wish the Russian Ambassador in Paris was ordered to approach the French Government with the request for a doctor's diploma for Philippe. Although the Republic was anxious to propitiate the powerful Russian ally, it was impossible for a civilized government to manufacture a doctor in this simple fashion. A way out was found: the Emperor ordered the Minister for War, who was the head of the Military Medical Academy in St. Petersburg, to deliver a doctor's certificate to Philippe. The Ukase was complied with and Philippe appeared at Court in the uniform of the Russian Army.

In 1902 Philippe had persuaded the Empress by his hypnotic methods that she was in a period of expectation. Neurotic women are open to such suggestions, when they exhibit even physical symptoms confirming them. For several months Court and society believed that a happy event was in store. At last real doctors were called in, who immediately saw that the Empress had made a mistake. This ridiculous incident did not destroy the influence of Philippe; to the general amazement he continued to enjoy the confidence of Alexandra and of Nicholas. He assured them that the effect of his treatment had been spoilt

by malevolent forces. He predicted that to have a
son it was necessary for the Empress to bathe at
midnight in the holy pool of St. Seraphim of Saroff.
Now it was true that a monk so named had lived at a
monastery at Saroff and had died in the odour of sanctity, but the Church had not proclaimed him a saint. It is
a mystery how Philippe came to know about the "saint,"
but his suggestion was sufficient for the Empress to
see that it was carried out. The Emperor sent for
Pobyedonostzeff, the Procurator of the Holy Synod.
The "Great Inquisitor," who had served three generations of autocrats and had been instrumental in estab-
lishing the theory of their unlimited power, protested,
nevertheless, when ordered to have Seraphim proclaimed a saint by the Orthodox Church. He pointed
out that this was a thing pertaining to the spiritual
side and that the Holy Synod, after mature examination and much prayer, could alone decide in the matter.
Nicholas did not contradict his old counsellor and the
latter left under the impression that he had been able
to prevent a foolish enterprise. But on the same day
Pobyedonostzeff received from his master a written
order to arrange for the proclamation of the new
saint in a year's time, "so as to give the Synod the
time necessary for examination and prayers." Thus,
by the will of a French charlatan, Seraphim was made
a saint of the Russian calendar. In the late summer
of 1903 Nicholas and Alexandra went on a pilgrimage
to Saroff, where, amid a great concourse of people,
the proclamation and glorification of Seraphim was

accomplished with all the splendour of an ancient ritual. At midnight the Empress descended to the pool and bathed in it as prescribed by Philippe. It is also true that in June of the next year a son was born to the Imperial pair. A miracle? A coincidence? The important thing is that in the eyes of Nicholas and Alexandra their son was the gift of St. Seraphim. Amid great rejoicings the child was given the name of Alexis, "the Man of God." What a triumph his birth was for Philippe!

But Philippe did not live long to enjoy his exalted position. In 1905, during a visit to his native town, where, as a good bourgeois, he had gone to attend to his investments, he suddenly died. The death was certified as natural by a medical practitioner, but the Empress believed that Philippe had been removed by heavenly intervention and was not dead. She treasured his memory and kept near her an icon, which Philippe had given her. A silver bell was attached to the icon and Philippe had promised that it would ring at the moment when an enemy approached the Empress or her husband. Alexandra had an absolute faith in this promise, as we can see from her letters. From the same source we learn that during the War Nicholas carried with him for luck a stick, which had belonged to Philippe.[3]

---

[3] In Nicholas' diary for July 20, 1905: "in the evening we received the sad news of Monsieur Philippe's death. Exactly on the day of Elias." This obscure reference to the Prophet Elias, who according to the legend was taken alive to heaven, is connected with some prophecy of Philippe and explains the faith of the Empress in his survival.

The Tragic Change

How great was the influence of Philippe over the mind of the Empress is proved by an inscription made by her in the diary of Nicholas on February 13, 1904, soon after the beginning of the fatal war with Japan:

> *Sweet Love, before taking the Holy Communion wifey asks you to forgive her for any word or deed of hers, which may have hurt you. Oh deary, what a comfort in this trying time to take the Lord's Supper together. May it give you strength and energy in your heavy task God has laid upon you—could I but help you. I can only pray with heart and soul for you and our beloved country. God and our dear Friend will help us. That I know. I kiss you fondly.*

It was a glorious day for the Empress when her boy was born. For twelve years she had waited and prayed. At last by the will of God, on the advice of "our friend" and with the help of St. Seraphim a miracle had been performed. Alexis Nicolayevitch, a lusty baby boy, lay in his cot in the room next to hers under the care of a competent English nurse. All was well and Alix could become again a normal young woman with a sensible outlook on things. Life was good indeed: her beloved Nicky was with her and the four dear daughters. And now there was Sunshine, the little son, the fulfilment of her ardent prayers, who would bring her back to health and make her the most popular woman in Russia. Life was Paradise!

But, when the boy was barely a month old, fate

intervened again. In the diary of Nicholas we read under the date of September 8, 1905:

> *Wednesday*. At 11 o'clock, drove to church with the girls. Alix and I were anxious about little Alexis' bleeding from the navel, which continued with intermittances until evening. It became necessary to send for Korovin [4] and for Fedoroff, the Surgeon; they put on a bandage at about 7 o'clock. The little one was remarkably quiet and gay. How awful it is to live through these minutes of anxiety. . . .

The attack, fortunately, was a slight one and two days later Nicholas was able to say that "the anxiety which gripped the heart" had departed and that his "soul was full of light." This was the first of the attacks of bleeding from which the little fellow was to suffer during his short life, throwing his parents each time into a state of heart-rending anguish. For the boy was a victim to the hereditary disease for which science has not yet found a remedy: haemophilia, which in certain families is transmitted through the females, who remain immune, to some of the males, who are condemned to perish. Their blood is deprived of the capacity to coagulate and an external cut, however slight, or an internal haemorrhage from a slight knock even, may have fatal consequences. The quantity of Hessian blood in his parents was dangerously great; the warning signs against consanguineous unions should have been taken into account, when the marriage was

---

[4] A well known doctor.

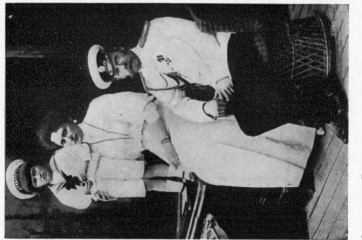

ALEXANDRA FEODOROVNA AND NICHOLAS II WITH THE CZAREVITCH ALEXIS, ON THEIR YACHT, THE "STANDARD," 1908

ALEXANDRA FEODOROVNA AND NICHOLAS II AS ANCIENT CZARINA AND CZAR AT COURT BALL AT WINTER PALACE

contemplated. By his long-drawn-out sufferings the boy paid for the mistaken marital policy of his ancestors.

From the letters of the Empress it is clear that the part played by heredity in the illness of her son was not clear to her. She certainly did not envisage the position as hopeless. She speaks of Alexis as the future Emperor, reigning long after his parents have returned to dust. Her anguish was all the greater at each new attack, for she always hoped that "this" attack would be the last and that the boy's health would be completely re-established. The harassing alternation of despair with hope, destined to be dashed to pieces again and again, wore Alexandra down mentally and physically. She sought refuge in the religious feeling, bordering on downright mania, by which she was dominated. She prayed to God for aid and believed that her prayer had been heard, when she met Rasputin.

German princesses, anxious to exchange their poor circumstances for the splendour of the Imperial Court, became converted to the Orthodox faith as a matter of convenience. Not so Alexandra: she accepted Orthodoxy only when she had brought herself to believe that, as a religion, it was superior to the one in which she had been born. It was natural that she should be inclined to attach importance to that side of her new faith which differed most from rationalistic Protestantism. This made her an easy victim to the eastern influences which create an atmosphere of illuminated mysticism in the Russian Church; it is saturated with the supernatural and the miraculous. To Russians, steeped therein from birth, the mystic ambience, with its cult of images, its spiritual appeal, and its defiance of logic, does no harm and often affords inspiration. For a young Protestant woman, suddenly immersed in this strange atmosphere, there is danger: she becomes drunk with the new spiritualistic wine. This happened to Alexandra; having discarded her western creed as an act of faith and not simply as a gesture of court etiquette, she became a devotee of Orthodoxy in its eastern aspect. If in her youth the only ornament above the head of her bed had been a verse from the Bible, she now worshipped before a wall full of icons with the faces of saints peering at her from between gold and silver ornaments, studded with jewels, while lamps burned before them day and night. To Alexandra these saints became a living presence!

In its pursuit of the mystical behind the formal exterior of the official church, the soul of the Russian people has always been susceptible to influences, emanating as if spontaneously from a divine inspiration. This explains the awed respect shown to "men of God," hermits and religious fanatics, who possess a faith based not on dogmas, but on sentiment and inner conviction. So exalted is the position of these beings that the ordinary measure of right and wrong does not apply; they may commit crimes without losing

their essential sanctity. This explains Rasputin—a
debauchee and a common criminal, who, possessed of
a mysterious spiritual power, remained a saintly person to his admirers. He was a Siberian peasant of
the name of Grigory Novihh, but the villagers called
him Rasputin [5] because of his immorality. Neurotic
ladies of society were under the spell of his magnetic
personality. The "black" grand duchesses were
among them; it was they who brought him to the Palace to replace the lamented Philippe. On November
1, 1904, Nicholas mentions briefly in his diary:

> To-day we made the acquaintance of Grigory,
> the Man of God, from the Province of Tobolsk.

Rasputin became a favourite of the Emperor and
Empress, whom he addressed with a rustic familiarity,
verging on rudeness, which they took to be the true
voice of the Russian people, pleasant to the ear, tired
by the adulatory phrases of the polished courtiers.
The wily peasant refrained from exhibiting his sen-
suality in the presence of the Imperial couple. He impressed them with the force of his religious convictions. They imagined to have found in the "Man
of God" a successor to their friend Philippe. Rasputin was an improvement on the latter, because he
was a Russian product representing the native soil.
The foundation of his power over the Empress was
her belief in his ability to save her boy from bleeding
to death. Rasputin professed to be able to arrest

---

[5] "Rasputin" means "depraved" in Russian.

the flow of blood from any wound. In Russia this is called *sagavarivat krov*—to bewitch the blood. The popular belief is that chosen people possess this peculiar gift. We leave it to scientists to discuss, if such a thing belongs to the domain of material possibility. We only say that the belief is spread in Russia and there are people who allege to have witnessed cases when it was accomplished. On one occasion Alexis had had an accident; he ruptured a small blood vessel. The bleeding was profuse and the doctors confessed their impotence. The distracted parents saw their son fading away before their eyes. Rasputin offered his services. He prayed over the boy and looked at him fixedly with his greenish-grey eyes. The flow of blood ceased as if by enchantment. Alexis was saved, but his mother was in the power of the intriguer. Grigory, the "Man of God," was to her a supernatural being. Each word of his, even a crass stupidity, was to Alexandra a divine revelation. Grigory declared that Alexis was safe, as long as he was near by to watch over him. Here is the origin of the power of Rasputin. His uncouth sayings announced the will of God. Russia was falling into the power of antichrist!

A mass of evidence exists, which shows that part at least of Rasputin's power was based on influence akin to hypnotism. That there was a strange force in his greenish-grey eyes we know by personal experience. The following extract from the diary of a lady is of interest as suggesting a hypnotic link between

Rasputin and the boy Alexis.[6] This lady came with
her sister-in-law from Moscow to make a desperate
attempt to save a relative arrested by the political
police. They managed to get at Rasputin, of whose
immense influence they had heard. Several times they
saw him at his house. Under the date of November
29, 1915, we read:

> We went to see him yesterday evening. There
> was nobody else. He gave the order to say that he
> was not at home. As we were going up the stairs
> I saw two detectives near the entrance. "Why is
> it that you are always watched by detectives?"
> "Certainly. I have so many enemies. To them I
> am like a cataract on the eye. They would be
> glad to get rid of me. But that's nonsense; their
> hands are too short for the job." "Tsarskoe
> loves you very much and takes care of you?"
> "Yes, both He and She love me. He loves me
> particularly. He cannot help himself: he must
> love and guard me. If I disappear, They will
> disappear too and Russia will be no more." I
> thought to myself with indignation that his
> self-confidence is unique. "Aha! you think that I
> am abominably confident? I know what you
> think. But, darling, I know what I am saying.
> As I have said—so it will be." I was confused.
> I am always astonished by his power of penetra-
> tion. Often he guesses my thoughts and says what
> I think. The maid called him to the telephone:
> "Tsarskoe calling." He approached [the tele-
> phone]: "Alesha cannot sleep? He has got a

---

[6] E. Djanumova, "Mov Vstretchy a Grigoryem Rasputinym," *Sovremenniya Sapisky,* XIV, 1923, Paris.

pain in his ear? Bring him to the telephone." A
gesture towards us imposing silence. "Alesha,
what is the meaning of this? Midnight and still
you are awake? It hurts? Nothing hurts. Lie
down immediately. The ear does not hurt. I
tell you: it does not hurt. Sleep, sleep at once.
Sleep, I tell you. Do you hear? Sleep." A quarter of an hour later the telephone rang again:
"Alesha's ear does not hurt any more. He is
sleeping peacefully. How did he go to sleep?"
"Why not? I told him to go to sleep." "But
he had a pain in his ear?" "But I told him that
the pain was gone." He spoke with calm confidence, as if it could not be otherwise.

Let us understand the position of Alexandra. To
have death at your elbow for weeks that draw out
into months, and for months which become years, is
a harrowing experience. The cruelty is intensified,
when death comes into the open, rattling its naked
horror, and then recedes again into the shadow—a
malignant presence. When death in this manner
menaces our best and dearest, life becomes martyrdom; nerves cannot resist the strain without breaking. Memoirs tell us how shocked people were by
the sight of the nervous state of the Empress, who
could not see any one she did not know intimately,
without experiencing physical pain. What the woman,
what the mother suffered we can only surmise! Light
comes from the book of M. Gilliard, who for thirteen years was tutor to the Imperial children and as
such obtained glimpses of the intimate life of the

family. Describing a terrible attack of bleeding, to which Alexis nearly succumbed during a stay at a hunting box in Poland, Gilliard [7] says:

I found myself in the corridor opposite Alexis Nicolayevitch's room, from which a moaning sound came distinctly to my ears. I suddenly noticed the Tsarina running up, holding her long and awkward train in her two hands. I shrank back against the wall, and she passed me without observing my presence. There was a distracted and terror-stricken look on her face. I returned to the dining room. The scene was of the most animated description. . . . Every one was laughing and exchanging jokes. The evening was at its height. A few minutes later the Tsarina came back. She had resumed the mask and forced herself to smile pleasantly at the guests who crowded round' her. But I had noticed that the Tsar, even while engaged in conversation, had taken up a position, from which he could watch the door, and I caught the despairing glance, which the Tsaritsa threw him as she came in. An hour later I returned to my room, still thoroughly upset at the scene, which had suddenly brought home to me the tragedy of this double life.

The unfortunate parents believed that for reasons of State they were obliged to maintain a pretence of gaiety, while their son was lying in the next room on the verge of death. They were afraid of compromising his future, if it became known that he was incapacitated by a dreadful illness. This double life, prolonged for more than ten years, was terrible. We

---

[7] *Thirteen Years at the Russian Court,* Pierre Gilliard, Hitchinson & Co., London.

are surprised that the character of the Empress did not alter more than it did, and that her health was not ruined to an extent greater than it was. When her child was brought to her—the handsomest baby imaginable, with lovely fair curls and great blue-grey eyes under a fringe of long curling lashes—the mother took him in her arms with the anguished thought: "Oh Lord, for how long?" In the calm intervals between the attacks Alexis looked a healthy child with a fresh pink colour and a bewitching smile. The mother fondled him, quaking inwardly, as she thought of the pallor of the same face, when the awful bleeding happened. Poor woman! Can we refuse her sympathy? It was natural for her to cling to Rasputin in her despair. When Russia was defeated by Japan and the revolutionary movement broke out openly threatening to engulf the throne and with it the existence of her beloved husband and the future of her son, she turned to the "Man of God" for advice. He was the prophet, through whom God spoke to fortify her resolve and that of Nicholas to fulfil the pact with heaven solemnly concluded at the coronation.

CHAPTER XII

AN IDEAL LOST

HE Russian Revolution began with a shot fired on January 6, 1905. The affair was and remains a mystery. On that day the Emperor came to St. Petersburg from Tsarskoe Selo to be present at the annual ceremony of the Blessing of the Waters. As he was standing in the chapel, open on all sides, specially erected for the occasion on the bank of the river Neva, in front of the Winter Palace, a salute was fired by a battery stationed on the bank opposite. One of the guns, instead of the blank cartridge with which it should have been loaded, discharged shrapnel straight at the chapel. There were several victims and the Dowager Empress, standing at the window of the Palace, watching the ceremony, was covered with glass splinters from the shattered panes. The incident was never cleared up. The battery was the Emperor's favourite one of the Guard Artillery and the officers were treated by him as personal friends. The men were picked soldiers. The secret societies, always keen on claiming responsibility for any attack against established authority, in this case kept silence. Yet the killed and wounded, and the windows shattered by the explosion were there to prove that the facts were real enough. Nicholas, with the fatalism characteristic of his nature, ordered the inquiry to be discontinued. The incident was forgotten in the terrible events which occurred three days later, on January ninth, when Gapon, the priest, led a mass of workmen to the Winter Palace in the hope of obtaining a hearing from the Emperor, only to be shot down by the troops.

In spite of the Great War and ensuing calamities the world has not altogether forgotten that day. It was the last occasion on which the people went to seek the Emperor, not to dethrone him, but to put their needs before him. The nature of the procession was misunderstood by the authorities, who, fearing a revolutionary outbreak, foolishly gave such orders to the military that shooting became inevitable. We are not writing the history of the reign of the last Russian Emperor and only place the ninth of January on record as the moment when the patience of the nation reached its breaking point. Events began to happen, which developed into an open revolutionary movement in the autumn of the same year. The Russian armies had suffered shameful defeats at the hands of the Japanese; their discipline was undermined by pacifist propaganda. Inside the country the administration, faced by the need of dealing with an economic and, worse still, with a moral crisis, displayed a pusillanimity and ineptitude which until then had only been suspected. The machine of autocracy, kept together so long by the force of inertia, was falling to pieces. Autocracy was going under not because it was proved to be bad for Russia, but because it was a bad autocracy and, as such, useless to Russia. In October, 1905, the nation rose, more in disgust than in anger, and by a general strike, punctuated with bloody risings and an outcrop of political murders, obliged the Emperor to capitulate. Nicholas conceded a democratically elected legislative assembly. The limitation of the autocratic power was vague and no cabinet was foreseen, responsible to the representatives of the people. But a part of the nation declared itself content and broke with the revolutionary groups, which, on the contrary, increased their activities so as to obtain full civic rights. The Portsmouth Treaty ended the war with Japan, and Witte, the great financier, obtained for the Government a large foreign loan. With a full exchequer and with no enemy threatening from outside Nicholas felt secure and began to curtail the liberties which he had been forced to concede. His policy caused a much more violent outbreak of the Revolution, but it seemed at the time that the Imperial Government had regained a major part of its prestige. To the Empress this period was a moral disaster, for she lost her faith in the infallibility of the political judgment of Nicholas. Convinced that autocracy in Russia was justified by the pact with heaven made at the coronation, she saw Nicholas bowing before the storm and not only diminishing his own position, but also endangering the heritage for their son.

Alexandra had dreamt of a glorious name in history for her husband. As far back as 1896 she had taken a vivid interest in the secret schemes discussed by the Imperial Government for an attack against Constantinople. It was proposed to put this ancient jewel, for centuries the object of Russian ambition, in the crown of Nicholas. The adventure did not pass beyond the stage of discussion: dreams followed of expansion in Asia. The fertile Mandjuria, already traversed by a Russian railway concession, was to become a province of the Empire. The same fate was prepared for Mongolia—a stepping stone towards Tibet. Corea was to be made a vassal state, under a Russian commissioner, and the battle fleet, based on the stronghold of Port Arthur, was to dominate the sea routes to Northern China. The Emperor of All the Russias would add to his titles that of Emperor of the East. A fine dream this, which Alexandra believed her beloved Nicholas to be man enough to accomplish. So absolute was the faith of the Imperial couple in the might of Russia and in the weakness of her adversaries that, when the war with Japan broke out, they never doubted the defeat of "these apemen." The author recollects how, in the first days of the war, when the enemy was hammering at the gates of Port Arthur, a set of regulations was published for the administration of Japanese territory, which would be occupied by the Russian forces.

An Ideal Lost

The dream vanished and the autocratic fabric in the country began to creak and grind ominously; for what seemed an endless time it tottered on the brink of destruction, and then by a stroke of luck was saved, for the time being at least. But in the eyes of Alexandra the prestige of Nicholas as a great ruler was shattered irreparably. She loved him dearly still, and, prompted by her love, perhaps more than by any other motive, she decided that, henceforward, she must co-operate to retrieve the fortunes of the dynasty. It became a favourite saying of hers that she "had breeches on." Alexandra wanted to be, and became, after 1905, an active partner of Nicholas in the work of government. The Princess Alix, who on her arrival in Russia was content to live in the shadow of her husband and to know of politics only as much as he wanted to tell her, had ceased to exist. The imperious woman, who now took her place, claimed a share of power. The influence of the Dowager Empress, who in the first years of the reign had stood as a trusty counsellor at the side of her son, was reduced to naught. The ministers, who often had heard from Nicholas the homely phrase: "I will consult Mother," now learnt that it was Alexandra who had the last word in everything.

Unfortunately, Alexandra was not prepared for the part of an autocrat. She was convinced, it is true, of the godly origin of autocratic power. She also possessed a strong will, but her brain was incapable of statesmanlike ideas, she had no knowledge, no experience, and she lacked the precious talent of making friends and choosing servants. These were the real obstacles on her road to power. The devoted Nicholas himself was but too glad to see his wife act as a real Empress before his adoring eyes. Alexandra sought guidance and she found it in her deep religious feeling, which had been transformed into a superstitious mania. She believed that God was particularly interested in the protection of the autocratic principle, because all democratic ideas were from the devil. It was necessary to know God's will exactly, so Rasputin became invaluable: was he not the "Man of God," sent to her by Providence to save and protect her child against death? Was he not in constant contact with heaven, which inspired his thoughts and formed the words he pronounced? Was he not the "friend" whose presence consolidated the throne and saved Russia from destruction?

The scandal of Rasputin's influence over the affairs of State had grown to such proportions that in January, 1912, a Conservative newspaper, the *Novoye Vremia,* broke the silence at last and denounced a "moujik, all knots and ugliness, with the face of an inebriate and with peculiar eyes," who "made and unmade bishops" and "who for personal revenge utilized relations in the highest circles." Rasputin was made the subject of an interpellation in the Douma and the Holy Synod was asked "to protect the sanctity of the Faith and the Throne against an adventurer." For a time Rasputin retired to his native village, but from there he continued to guide the thoughts of Alexandra and, when the noise of the scandal had died down, he returned to St. Petersburg and when the War broke out he was installed as the master of the destinies of Russia.

No doubt in the years which came after the Russo-Japanese War the Empress Alexandra was an ardent partisan of the reactionary measures intended to reduce the scope of civil freedom, which Nicholas "in his weakness" had been forced to concede in 1905. The statesman, and the great Witte above all, who had seen the need for Constitutional reform, were considered by her as personal enemies. She pursued them with an implacable hatred. She became the chief backer of the infamous "Union of the Russian People," in which a few Monarchists were blended with common criminals and police officials. She permitted her name with that of the Emperor to be inscribed on the roll of this organization, which, as the land soon came to know, was responsible for *pogroms* and outrages of all sorts. It is this connection with the Union, which finally separated the nation from its sovereigns. It was intolerable to see common criminals taking part in *pogroms* one day, condemned to prison by the courts on the next and then immediately pardoned by their Imperial master. Alexandra, naturally, ignored the criminal side and saw only the passionate demonstrations of loyalty, in which the members of the Union indulged to deserve the Imperial bounty and to cover up the tracks of their lawless activities.

The Tragic Bride

Let us remember that the woman before us was ill. We are acquainted with the state of mortal terror in which Alexandra lived for years. From her mother she had inherited a highly sensitive disposition and her physical health had been delicate from youth. Nicholas tells us in his diary that as a young girl she suffered already from pains and was easily fatigued. In her letters there is sufficient material for a medical man to come to the conclusion that the health of Alexandra was seriously impaired before she was forty and that her nerves were in a state which there would be moderation in describing as tense. President Poincaré in his memoirs supplies evidence on this point. His first visit to Russia was in 1912 as Minister for Foreign Affairs. M. Poincaré upon arrival was taken almost immediately to the Palace of Peterhoff, on the coast of the Finnish Gulf, the residence in which the Imperial family spent the hottest part of summer. The visitor was taken to a drawing room to await the Emperor and Empress, who were out driving in the park.*

In the expectation of the arrival of the Emperor, I went up to the windows, which look out upon the terrace. I watched the cascades. . . . I was absorbed by the contemplation of the view, when an open carriage drawn by a pair of prancing horses came to a halt in front of the chief palace entrance. The Emperor and the Empress descended from it. They came from the Villa Alexandria, their modest residence, two kilometres away. The face of Nicholas II

---

*R. Poincaré, *Au Service de la France*, II, 1926.

was bronzed by the cruise in Finnish waters, during which he had met the Kaiser. . . . The Empress had on a dress of dark hue; a large hat trimmed with lace and decorated by a large black ostrich feather threw a shadow over her somewhat pointed features. The Master of Ceremonies came up and led me through room after room to the private apartments, where Nicholas II and the Empress, standing side by side, were expecting me. The audience lasted for about half an hour and during all this time they did not invite me to sit down and themselves remained immobile and standing. Two years later, when I came as President of the Republic my reception was quite different, but in 1912 etiquette dealt severely with me. However the Emperor treated me with the utmost distinction. . . . At his side the Empress remained motionless like a statue. But after a few minutes she took part by moving her head to accentuate the remarks of the Emperor and she put in a few discreet remarks of her own. From time to time a red flush spread suddenly over her face and it looked as if she felt a pain stab at her heart, or had difficulty to breathe.

Two years later M. Poincaré returned again to Russia a few weeks before the beginning of the great tragedy of the War. M. Paléologue, the French Ambassador at the Russian Court, relates in his memoirs [1] the story of his visit. One evening Nicholas came with his wife and daughters on board of the battleship in which M. Poincaré had come to Russia. For some time the Emperor and the President retired to the lat-

---

[1] Maurice Paléologue, *La Russie des Czars.*

ter's apartments to discuss affairs of State. The Empress remained sitting on deck with the Ambassador in respectful attendance. M. Paléologue was struck by the sudden change which came over the features of Alexandra: they became drawn and showed intense nervous agitation. By a sign, as if unable to speak, the Empress indicated that the band playing near her exasperated her. The music was immediately stopped. The eldest daughter of Alexandra, who had been sitting at a distance carefully watching her, approached, exchanged a few words with her mother and then told the Ambassador that he was requested to remain sitting next to the Empress, who was greatly obliged to him for his kindness in so quickly stopping the noise. After a painful interval of strained silence the Emperor returned on deck and took his wife home immediately. War clouds were soon to cover the horizon of Europe and this poor woman was destined to exercise authority over the fortunes of the largest empire in the world!

CHAPTER XIII

RASPUTIN

N unwritten rule protects the reader of an historical work against the intrusion of the writer's personality. This is fair, because the impact of the personal element tends to substitute sentiment for reason, and impression for facts. For once, in this chapter, the author breaks with this polite rule by giving a glimpse of his personal feelings. A point has been reached in the story when the subject of Rasputin cannot be avoided any longer. In addition to the material obtained at first hand the author possesses the results of direct observation, but the pen, already put to paper, has been lifted time and again, and phrases ready to be poured out have been left unsaid; so great is the feeling of repulsion at the thought of a distasteful subject. Rasputin, as a factor in history, and Rasputin, as a case for the pathologist, we discuss calmly, but they cannot be separated from Rasputin, the product of a mysterious spiritualism and Rasputin, the crapulous debauchee. To reach vital evidence in this post mortem the scalpel works through a purulent mass and a spasm of revulsion runs down the spine of the investigator. A feeling of nausea overcomes the author, when his thought, projected towards the important points, is held up by an entanglement of disgusting details. The repulsion is enhanced by the fact that at the same time there is a peculiar unhealthy attraction in the subject: the sort of attraction, which the work of Satan exercises even over strong-minded people. In the olden days it was exorcised by a solemn: *vade retro Satanas.*

In the case of Rasputin the difficulty is to discover the lines of division between the several personalities by which his physical body was inhabited. Of this multiplicity there is little doubt. The easy way is to declare that the man was an impostor, professing to have supernatural powers, in which people, who knew of his favour at Court, made a show of believing. Yet we know that he had followers who believed in him implicitly, long before he became known to the Empress and to her husband. These faithful followers extracted him from his Siberian village, brought him to St. Petersburg and recommended him to Nicholas and Alexandra. We have known disinterested women, ay, and men, who, when he was at the height of his power, venerated in Rasputin the "Man of God" without any thought about personal advancement. These fanatics became the victims of unscrupulous adventurers, who used them as instruments for carrying out their contemptible schemes. This circumstance cannot alter the fact of Rasputin's sanctity in the eyes of many. Rasputin himself was convinced of his gift of supernatural power and was sincere when he spoke about his own proximity to God. In its superb impudence this faith in himself was so amazing that it became impregnated with an element of greatness. Rasputin did not think for a moment that his dissolute morals, gross vices and bestial acts should deprive him of the "seal" of God's elect. On the contrary, the abominations which he practised, to his distorted imagination, in a mysterious way, were milestones on the road to spiritual perfection and salvation.

The western mind has drawn a clear line between good and evil and makes a peremptory distinction between virtue and vice. But in the eastern atmosphere permeating Russian life all is vague; the divides are tortuous and often disappear altogether. The Russian mind is pervaded with doubt—a soul-searching criticism without rhyme or reason—an enemy of all established things. Good is opposed to evil? Good is from God? But what is good, what is evil? If all is from God, then evil is from him too? From doubt to paradox and from the paradox to defiance of accepted views, the tormented Slav soul soars up to nerve-shattering heights or is thrown down into deep abysses. Add to this a gift of imagination and the scene will be set for strange happenings. No other explanation is needed of the origin of Bolshevism in Russia; the dogmas of Marx form the outer crust, while beneath is the anarchy of a storm-swept soul. There can be no surprise if under such conditions the Orthodox faith, an intrinsic part of the national existence, is covered with sectarian excrescences. Of these the strangest is, no doubt, the sect of the Khlysty, who believe that sexual depravation is the crowning summit of religious ecstasy. It is proved that Rasputin from his youth was a member of this sect of sexual dervishes.

Among the hard-bitten Siberian peasants of his own village in the province of Tobolsk Rasputin could not become a powerful personage. For they had known him since childhood and had witnessed his misdeeds, among which figured horse stealing—a crime particularly hateful to a rural population. But in the neighbouring monastery, which he often visited, there was a holy icon, which attracted a great number of pilgrims. It happened that the pious wife of a rich merchant from the provincial town—one of those simple-minded women, who in the olden days were the chief supporters of religion—came under the spell of Rasputin's greenish eyes and acknowledged him as the "Man of God." Thus was founded a career destined to make Rasputin the most powerful man in Russia. The superstitious woman took the wonder worker to her town and introduced him to her friends. His fame grew apace, travelling ahead of him; not only women, who were his natural prey, but stolid men and even bishops believed in his sanctity. Passing from one circle of admirers to another Rasputin rose swiftly in society and, after a few years, we find him installed as an oracle in St. Petersburg, an idol and the source of religious ecstasy for the wives of ministers and ladies of the Court. Rasputin accepted this elevation as a thing due to his greatness and not to luck. This superb confidence only stimulated the faith in him and the zeal of his devotees.

Among the women enslaved to the will of Rasputin was the young Anna Virubova, the friend of the Empress. She was the daughter of M. Taneeff, the faithful servant of three emperors, as chief of the private secretariat. Anna, when yet a child, became known to the Empress who admired her blonde cherubic beauty. In the eyes of the little girl was a world of innocence, the sort of innocence, which, when people grow up, is transformed into a doltish stupidity. The sweet child looked up to the lovely Empress with adoration. Once, when Anna was very ill, the Empress came to see her; the visit coincided with the crisis after which the health of the patient swiftly began to improve. Anna believed that the white apparition had saved her life. Her adoring respect for the Empress became a dog-like devotion. The mystically inclined Alexandra was ready to be persuaded that heaven willed her to take care of the girl. To establish her in life she made her marry a smart officer of the Imperial yacht. Anna's heart was given elsewhere, but she obeyed the Imperial order. The marriage turned out to be a terrible mistake and was annulled soon after. The Empress, blaming herself for the match, became more than ever fond of Anna and made of her a friend and confidante. The young woman, whose insignificant personality is reflected in the memoirs which she has published, became the victim of a religious sentimentalism, which made her an easy prey to Rasputin. We know from the letters of the Empress, how near Anna was to the Imperial family. She was treated more like a daughter than a lady of the Court. Alexandra scolded her for her stupidity and called her behind her back "the fat cow," but the thought of separating herself from her never arose, even when the caprices of Anna filled her mistress with deep anger. For Anna was the faithful messenger between the "Man of God" and the Empress. Her poor brain was obliged to memorize—and with what difficulty—the sayings of Rasputin to be faithfully repeated at the Palace. That the influence of Rasputin over Anna was only spiritual was proved when the Commission of Inquiry, set up after the Revolution by the Provisional Government in its desire to penetrate to the heart of things, tore away the veil from intimate secrets. Anna was the slave of Rasputin and his tool. During the War a train in which she was travelling from St. Petersburg to Tsarskoe Selo left the rails and was overturned. She was taken out of the débris and the doctors, working over her shattered body, said that there was no hope. The distracted Empress sent for Rasputin, who came and stood over Anna and cried her name in her ear. She came out of the deep faint, in which she had lain for hours, and her health mended quickly. A shortened leg remained to remind her of the catastrophe. Tapping along the passages of the Palace with her stick,

Anna resumed her duties as the mouthpiece of Rasputin.

The Empress could not bear to have Rasputin at too great a distance from the Court; he was to remain near in case his intervention were needed to save the Czarevitch. The "Man of God" became a regular resident of St. Petersburg. With him came his wife, a son and two daughters, but them we mention in passing, because they have no part in the story. For long periods Rasputin's family was sent back to the native village, where they led the dull life of the ordinary peasants. More important in the existence of Rasputin were the two women, Dunya and Kilina. Dunya was an elderly Siberian rustic—cook, maid, secretary and adviser all in one. She had known Rasputin all her life, treated him with scanty respect and went about the flat undismayed by the aristocratic admirers who filled it. Kilina was a nun whom Rasputin had seduced. She had attached herself to his person, following him about wherever he went, carrying out the duties of secretary and doorkeeper. People who wanted to obtain an interview with Rasputin addressed themselves either to Dunya or to Kilina. The two women were the intermediaries through whom he received monetary offerings.

To a stranger Rasputin's flat seemed a madhouse. Having passed on the stairs a couple of detectives, sent by the Government to watch over the personal safety of the Imperial favourite, the visitor penetrated into a dark musty-smelling hall, where his coat was taken from him often not by a servant, but by one of the smart ladies, who considered it a worthy act to carry out menial duties in the house of the "Man of God." The waiting room beyond the hall was full of people from early morning until late at night. The whole of Russia seemed to be represented there: peasants in leather jerkins and in high boots, smelling of earth and dung, sat in a corner, looking with amazement at the company assembled, while their toil-hardened hands closed around bundles of documents which they had brought to show to the "Man of God," "who could speak to the Czar." Next to them, an officer of the Guards in his splendid uniform, humbly awaiting his turn. Portly village priests sat monumentally immobile with beards spread over their fat chests, on which great crosses hung on massively linked chains. A few students were there also with some request. But most of the people in the waiting room were women: peasants and nobles, women in homespun and in dresses from Paquin; girls with an exalted expression on their faces and elderly women, full of a holy enthusiasm. A lady in deep mourning clutched a small child to her bosom keeping her tear-filled eyes fixed on the door leading to the inner apartments. The room was full of noise. People talked loudly. In a corner a famous sculptor listened to the chatter of a popular journalist.

A fat individual with a vulgar expression on his ugly face comes in, apparently in a great hurry. He is the chairman of a great bank. Catching Dunya, as she hurries through the room, he presses a note in her hand and is admitted by her into the inner apartments. Meanwhile the telephone bell is ringing madly; the front door opens and shuts continuously; messengers arrive with baskets, large parcels and with bouquets of flowers.

In the badly lighted room, Rasputin sits at the head of the large table with its not too clean table-cloth and a large, not too well polished *samovar,* flanked by a battery of glasses and gaily painted tea-cups. A bunch of hothouse blooms in a cheap glass jar stands in the centre of the table and there are flowers on the mantelpiece and all over the modestly furnished room. Rasputin is surrounded by a company of feminine admirers. They are a mixed lot. Next to the titled wife of a famous general, all in silk, velvet and diamonds, sits a little old lady, who, judging by her antique dress, has arrived straight from the wilds of Siberia. Kilina is serving out tea to the ladies, who hold the glasses towards Rasputin. With dirty fingers he takes pieces of sugar from the bowl and drops them into the tea: in this manner the tea becomes blessed. The ladies devoutly kiss his hand. He drinks freely of his favourite Madeira wine. Anna Virubova comes in, straight from Tsarskoe Selo, with a portfolio full of papers. She refuses to sit down and says that she will attend to the people waiting to see the "Father." The latter proposes that the company should sing in chorus; Kilina leads off, the others take up the melody and the "Man of God" joins in with his deep bass. The singing is interrupted by the entry of a smart young man, who reminds Rasputin that it is time to leave for the fashionable restaurant, where in a private room a company of business men wants to discuss with him a Government contract. The ladies get up to leave; they kiss Rasputin's hand; he embraces and kisses them on the lips. He distributes black rye biscuits, which are devoutly wrapped up in fine lace handkerchiefs and put away in the handbags. Dunya produces untidy brown-paper parcels; these are snatched from her hands by the ladies. If opened they would be found to contain dirty body shirts of the "Man of God"; to wear them brings health and luck: the "dirtier the luckier." Rasputin remains alone for a few minutes with Anna; she comes from the Empress, who desires advice on a question of State. Rasputin sits in a majestical pose with his unkempt beard spread out over the breast of the shirt of pure white silk, which he ordinarily wears with a belt of knotted silk rope. His taloned fingers play with the long grey hairs, while his eyes look into the distance and from his lips fall words of Delphic wisdom, which Anna, listening with rapt attention, tries to enshrine in her memory, so as to report them exactly to her Imperial mistress. Dunya comes in bringing the *armyak,* the coat of the Russian peasant. Rasputin's *armyak* is made of the finest cloth and is lined with woven gold, while the collar and trimmings are of precious sable. A tall cap of the same fur completes the attire of Rasputin, who majestically descends to the motor car, in which several richly dressed men have been patiently waiting for his pleasure. They drive to an exclusive restaurant, where in a private dining room a sumptuous feast has been prepared. Rasputin is on his good behaviour; he drinks a lot, but his gestures are restrained and he pays careful attention to the scheme which a banker unfolds, while discreet Tartar waiters glide in and out, bringing new dishes and fresh bottles. Rasputin's comments are shrewd, but soon his mood changes and he demands that the Tziganies should be called in. A few minutes later these make their appearance—one of the famous gipsy choirs, whose orientalized songs have delighted Russians for generations—the women sit in a row on chairs in front, while the male singers stand behind them; their swarthy faces and flashing eyes betray a southern origin which centuries of existence in a cold climate have not been able to extinguish. With his head in his hands Rasputin sits at the table, listening to the mellow voices of the singers. Suddenly he jumps up and orders the gipsies to sing his favourite dancing song. They comply and Rasputin darts into the centre of the room and begins to dance. Gone is the apathy of a few minutes ago; his eyes blaze and his movements are amazingly nimble. He shouts wildly and gulps down glass after glass of his favourite Madeira. The singing grows shriller and Rasputin spins round and round like a great top whipped into frenzied action by the power of the wild music. He seizes a plate and, whooping, throws it at a shining mirror, which cracks and rains tinkling splinters on the floor. As the night advances the room fills itself; well known people and complete strangers crowd in to see the "Man of God" letting himself go; police officers stand discreetly behind the door in the passage, ready to intervene if the scandal becomes too great and, especially, if protection is needed by Rasputin. The latter behaves like a madman: his face is deadly pale and the staring eyes are pools of vice. He dances as if possessed, throwing himself from time to time on the sofa to toss off a tumblerful of the strong wine. In the early hours of the morning Kilina comes running: a messenger has arrived from Tsarskoe Selo, the "Father" is wanted there as soon as possible. Rasputin shouts a refusal: "Let her wait," but the guests surround him and press him to go to take a rest. He resists, but the handsome woman, one of the several who have slipped into the room, takes him by the hand and coaxes him to leave with her. Flinging an arm round her shoulders, he stumbles towards the door, stamping to the rhythm of the song of the gipsies and shouting blasphemies, which the public present hears in silence. But Rasputin suddenly has an idea. With uncertain steps he returns to the wine-splashed, disorderly table. From a pocket the "Man of God" produces a small bottle of ordinary glass; with an unsteady hand, pouring quantities of wine on the table, he fills it with Madeira and

Photograph by Wasserman, Moscow, Paris

RASPUTIN

with a wink, addressed to those sitting around, Rasputin replaces the bottle in his pocket. After this he leaves for good, half supported by his companion and singing a ribald song at the top of his powerful voice. But in a few hours Rasputin with his marvellous power of recuperation will be driving in a swift motor car to Tsarskoe Selo, as fresh as if, instead of wine, song and women, he had had a long and peaceful night's rest.

Rasputin was received at the Palace itself, but the Empress preferred meeting him in the quiet of the tiny drawing room of the unpretentious house which she had given to Anna Virubova quite near to the Palace gates. The evidence we possess shows that in the presence of his Imperial client the "Man of God" maintained a perfect decorum. His manners were restrained and he placed a curb on his language, abstaining from coarse or blasphemous remarks. His conduct was that of a benevolent rustic. He addressed the Empress (and the Emperor) with the intimate "Thou" but his familiarity was that of a devoted friend. And it is as of a friend that the Empress thought of him. In her letters the expression "Friend" and "our Friend" are met with all the time. The neurotic Alexandra obtained appeasement from her long conversations with her "friend." He spoke so calmly and simply and with such confidence! She did not understand all his cryptic sentences, but it was comforting for her to commune with a being so near to God. The "friend" had saved her son and his presence was a safeguard against further danger to that precious life. But the "friend" was also so wisely inspired; his advice was invaluable on all important issues. Alexandra in her stilted Russian would expose to her "friend" the problems which troubled the mind of the hard-worked Nicholas and it is true that sometimes Rasputin with his healthy peasant outlook on life and his knowledge of conditions inside Russia could give better advice than a minister, sealed up all his life in a bureaucratic St. Petersburg. Appointments to posts of importance were discussed with "our Friend," who recommended some candidates and warned against others. The first were usually those who were his admirers and the others those who treated him with contempt.

Rasputin, remembering his promise to the bankers, did not forget to ask the Empress to see that her husband approved the financial scheme which his friends had presented. When they had disposed of current "business" the conversation in Anna's drawing room veered towards religion, a theme in which the Empress was deeply interested and about which her "friend" spoke impressively. The face of Alexandra was suffused with the light of a great contentment, the painfully contracted corners of her mouth relaxed, her eyes became less fixed and the expression on her face rejuvenated. Rasputin talked away as if singing a lullaby. From religious questions he passed to a description of the beauty of the life of a hermit in the Siberian wilds; he described trees and flowers and promised Alexandra that some day he would show her his native village in Siberia where life was simple, free and near to God. She listened enraptured and kissed his dirty hand, while he muttered a blessing over her head. Anna came in to remind the Empress that she was due at the Palace to give audience to several highborn ladies. A look of pain came into the eyes of Alexandra, she rose reluctantly and her lips were compressed into a thin line. Her "friend" told her to be of good heart and promised that all would be well. As he was about to leave the room he suddenly returned and, producing a small bottle filled with a brown liquid from his pocket, he gave it to the Empress with a solemn assurance that the wine in the bottle had the property of bringing luck to the person who partook of it. Alexandra accepted the precious flask in her outstretched hands and then pressed her lips to it: the granddaughter of Queen Victoria had come to believe in the power of charms. When Nicholas was at the War, Alexandra, to preserve him against evil and to bring him luck, sent him various objects blessed by Rasputin. On January 11, 1916, she wrote:

"Now don't think me mad for my wee bottle, but our Friend sent her [Anna] one from his nameday feast and we each took a sip and I poured this out for you—believe it's Madeira. I swallowed for his sake—like Medicine—you do it too, please, though you dislike it. Pour it into a glass and drink it all up for his health, as we did."

Nicholas, immersed in the conduct of the war operations, found time to telegraph back nevertheless:

"Heartfelt thanks for the letters and the wee bottle."

and also wrote:

"My little Dove, I thank you heartily for your dear letter and also for the bottle and the flower from our Friend. I drank the wine straight from the bottle for his health and welfare—drank all to the last drop."

On another occasion, on June 14, 1915, the Empress had written:

"I send you a stick—a fish holding a bird—which was sent to Him from New Athos [1] to give to you. He used it first and now sends it to you as a blessing. If you can, use it sometimes. It would be nice. I rejoice to think it will be in your compartment near to the one M. Philippe touched."

Alexandra firmly believes in Rasputin's supernatural powers. She is convinced that he can influence even climatic conditions. So on December 22, 1915, she writes:

"Our Friend is always praying and thinking of the War. He says we are to tell him at once if anything particular happens. She [Anna] told Him about the fog [2] and he scolded, because he was not told at once. He says that no more fogs will disturb."

---

[1] A famous convent in the Caucasus on the Black Sea coast.

[2] Nicholas had written complaining of the difficulty of carrying on military operations in the prevailing fog.

In spite of the charlatanism of Rasputin, a charlatanism which he exhibited because he saw how it impressed his followers, we persist in saying that the man not only had an absolute faith in his nearness to God, but was possessed of powers the exact nature of which we cannot fathom. The following incident related by a trustworthy witness is an instance of the mysterious happenings.[3]

Madame Djanumova, a lady from Moscow, had made the acquaintance of Rasputin during the War. Her close relatives were being persecuted by the authorities for their supposed German connexion and Madame Djanumova was told by her friends that only Rasputin with his influence at Court, was in a position to help her. Her hope was deceived, because she refused to pay the price which the fellow demanded of her for his services. Nevertheless, for some time under the spell of his personality, she was a visitor at his flat and had opportunities to observe what was going on. She was accompanied on several occasions by a sister-in-law, who corroborates her evidence.

Madame Djanumova's niece was a delicate child. When in her case scarlet fever occurred simultaneously with diphtheria accompanied by pneumonia and kidney trouble, the doctors gave up hope. The telegram announcing the dreadful news arrived at the moment when Madame Djanumova was leaving the hotel to go to the flat of Rasputin. With his uncanny intuition

---

[3] Djanumova, "Moy Vstrechy a Grigoryem Rasputinym," *Sovremenniya Sapisky*, XIV, 1923.

the latter immediately saw that something was wrong. When told the bad news he took his visitor by the hand. Says Madame Djanumova:

Something strange happened for which I have no explanation. I cannot say what it was. He took me by the hand; his face became different; it was like that of a dead man—yellow, waxlike and immobile: terrible. The eyeballs rolled upwards so that only the whites were to be seen. He fiercely tugged at my hands and repeated in a dull voice: "She shall not die, she shall not die, she shall not die." After this he let go my hands, his face regained its colouring and he talked of other things, as if nothing had happened. . . . In the evening I got a telegram: "Alice better, temperature falling." . . . I went and showed the telegram to Rasputin, "Did you help really?" I asked, though naturally I did not believe it. He answered quite seriously: "But I told you that she would get well again." "Then try again and she will become quite well." "Little fool, how can I? That was not from me but from above. It cannot be repeated. But do not worry: I have said already that the child will be well." . . . I shall never forget his face, when he held my hands: it was that of a dead man and I shudder, when I think of it.

CHAPTER XIV

AGAIN RASPUTIN

HE power of Rasputin over the Empress cannot be understood if the fact is not taken into account that from first to last there was no question of money between them. After the Revolution the Commission of Inquiry, instituted by the Provisional Government, investigated the facts, and the Bolsheviks, when they came into power, continued the work in their desire to expose the evils of the Imperial régime. The mass of evidence so obtained does not furnish a single proof of the Empress or the Emperor having supplied Rasputin with funds. On the contrary, it is established that the money which flowed into the pocket of the "Man of God" came from quite different sources.

Nicholas and Alexandra led a sheltered life which made money unnecessary. They did not shop, buy tickets or pay bills; they had not even the occasion of giving a penny to a beggar; the Emperor did not carry a pocket book and the Empress had no purse. In her youth Alexandra had known the worries of a limited allowance, but after her marriage these had become a thing of the past. In her letters to Nicholas

she discusses the problems of their domestic life, but
money is not mentioned, except when she speaks of
large sums in connexion with charity or with affairs
of State. The influence of Rasputin was so powerful
because he refrained from asking favours for himself.
When his son was in danger of being called up as a
reservist during the War, Rasputin did his utmost to
prevent this. Even then he did not ask for a favour;
he struck an attitude of personal disinterestedness and
advised against the calling up of the class of the reserve
to which his son belonged under the pretext that it
was needed for work in the fields. Rasputin was
clever and understood that it was to his advantage
to consolidate his moral ascendency over the sovereigns by avoiding to ask for material advantages;
thereby he obtained all the more from his admirers
and, especially, from the people who needed his assistance in their dealings with government departments.
Even so, Rasputin did not accumulate great wealth,
as he could easily have done, and it is certain that
money was not his principal object in life and that he
spent immediately the major part of all he received.

It is a pity that in their unworldliness the Emperor
and Empress never gave a thought to the material
well being of their "Friend," it is a thousand pities
that they did not encourage him to take all he wanted
from the Treasury. The outcry would have been
loud, but Rasputin would not have become the associate of shady financiers, the connexion with whom
became a national danger during the War. This con-

nexion was brought about by the absence of legality in Russia under the Imperial régime. The law could be transgressed with impunity if the right channel to obtain patronage was discovered. The prostitution of the will and conscience of the people had for result the prevalence of the idea that "laws were there to be broken." As Rasputin was quite evidently the best channel to advance personal interests, even if they were opposed to regulations and, especially, if they were so opposed, the boldest law breakers became his friends. With his perverted attitude towards good and evil Rasputin was attracted by people of the same frame of mind. Also he needed money and where could he find it easier than in the backyard of the financial world?

The Bolsheviks in their poisonous hate of the Romanoffs are not content to raise against the latter accusations based on the solid evidence of which there is a superabundance. They want to prove that, in addition to having been misguided and foolish people, Nicholas and Alexandra were traitors to Russia. To prove the betrayal a book has been produced under official patronage in Moscow[1] which represents a strenuous effort to prove that the Empress, with the knowledge of Nicholas, worked to prepare the way for a separate peace between Russia and the Central Powers. The utmost which is proved, however, is that Alexandra did maintain a correspondence with

---

[1] Semennikoff, *Politika Romanovihh Nakanune Revolutzyy*, Moscow, 1926.

her brother, the Grand Duke of Hesse, who in his letters tried to pave the way towards a better feeling between the two Governments, but there is no evidence that his sister encouraged in him the slightest hope of success in this direction. On the contrary, we know from her letters that with perfect loyalty she stood by Nicholas, who had solemnly sworn not to separate his cause from that of the Allies. Although called *Niemka* by the Russians, Alexandra did not consider herself a German at all. She was a good Russian according to her lights, unfortunately her lights were bad. Prince Max, the heir to the Grand Duchy of Baden and the last Chancellor of William II, in his indigestible but valuable book [2] alludes to the attempts made from the German side to maintain relations during the War with the members of the Russian Imperial family, who were Germans by birth. He does not say all he knows, but it is clear that nothing of importance was achieved. On the contrary, the "German" grand duchesses were afraid to lift a finger to help their erstwhile country in any way, even when they wished to do so. As to the Empress, her name is not even mentioned!

The Bolshevik "historian" not being able to convict the Empress herself tries to achieve his object by proving the connexion between Rasputin, who dominated her, and the leading Germanophiles in St. Petersburg. The Bolsheviks, where German intervention in Russia is concerned, are competent witnesses, for was

[2] Prinz Max von Baden, *Erinnerungen und Dokumente,* Berlin, 1927.

it not their nearness to Hindenburg's General Staff
which permitted them to return to Russia in 1917?
In their desire to condemn the Empress through Rasputin they make out a strong case against the latter's
friends in the financial world of being the abettors
and spies of Germany. In fact, they show that during
the War the Germans were able to a great extent to
use Rasputin for obtaining valuable information. It
seems that some of the financiers with whom he was
on intimate terms were German agents. They met the
"Man of God" regularly several times in the week
and over a glass of wine extracted from him valuable
information which he had been given by the Empress
herself. She communicated items of military news
to Rasputin because she wanted his advice and his
prayerful intercession. Rasputin himself never seems
to have suspected what use was made of his indiscreet
remarks at the convivial dinner table. That the Empress was an innocent victim is proved by the amazing
fact, disclosed in the Bolshevik publication, that the
German General Staff was informed even of the time-
table to which the Imperial train was run behind the
front. In her letter of November 3, 1915, Alexandra writes:

"He [3] has brought me your secret [4] itineraries and
I shall not say a word about them to anybody, except
our Friend, so that he should guard you everywhere."

---

[3] The Minister of the Interior Chwostoff, who had been to see
Nicholas at Headquarters.
[4] The word "secret" is underlined in the letter.

The Tragic Bride

In the minutes of the Commission of Inquiry, among the evidence taken down from Beletzky, who had been Director of Police, stands the following statement:

The movements of Nicholas II were known in Germany; the itineraries of the Imperial trains were known there. So in November, 1915, when the Tsar and the Tsarevitch were going to the front, the Intelligence of the Western front communicated that a German aeroplane would throw a bomb on the line beyond Bachmatch. The train was to come from the station of Sarny. The Germans had information about the itineraries of the Imperial trains, the hours even, as I had occasion to discover later. . . . But the unexpected happened: the Tsarevitch began to bleed from the nose and the train, having turned back, was dispatched immediately towards Tsarskoe. At the same hour at the point indicated a German aeroplane from a great height bombed the auxiliary train, which precedes that of the Emperor.

When Beletzky made this statement to the Commission of Inquiry he could not have known that a telegram existed in which Nicholas informed his wife of the sudden change in his plans:

ALL DAY ALEXIS AS A RESULT OF A COLD HAS HAD INTERMITTENT BLEEDING FROM THE NOSE. ON THE ADVICE OF THE DOCTOR HAVE DECIDED TO RETURN TO HEADQUARTERS. I SHALL BE GLAD IF YOU WILL ARRIVE TO PASS DECEMBER 6TH TOGETHER. I EMBRACE YOU HEARTILY. NICHOLAS.

This telegram, discovered by Bolshevik investigators much later, was sent from a station on the railway less than an hour's travel from the Bachmatch mentioned by Beletzky.

The Bolsheviks in great detail explain that the headquarters of the German spying in Russia were connected with the offices of a great electrical enterprise, financed from Berlin, which possessed power stations in Moscow, St. Petersburg and other cities. We are in a position to supplement this information by the fact, withheld in the Bolshevik publication, that the company in question was under the management of the late Krassin, the right-hand man of Lenin, who at the time was masquerading as a *bona fide* servant of capital. During the War efforts were made by patriotic Russians to obtain the sequestration of this concern, but they came to nothing. A special commission was even constituted to take measures against the predominant position of German capital in Russian industrial undertakings. But, as the same Krassin by a trick of legerdemain was made a member, we can understand why the activities of the Commission were paralyzed from the beginning: a good example of the close connexion between German and Bolshevik interests, a connexion which has endured after the War in the form of the co-operation between the German junker and the communist of Moscow.

The same example proves that Alexandra could not have been a conscious accomplice. By no effort of a distorted imagination is it possible to admit an intention on her part to promote the cause of Germany by endangering the life of her own beloved husband and son. We are inclined to believe also that Rasputin was the unconscious tool of a powerfully organized intelligence service. This is confirmed by a statement made to the Commission of Inquiry by Chwostoff, who had been Minister for the Interior and who, as such, was well informed about all that was going on in the Rasputin circle:

Rasputin was a visitor in Tsarskoe and R.[5] asked him to find out if there would be an advance or not? R. explained that he wanted to have this information to decide if he should buy up forests in the Minsk province [behind the front]. For if an advance was planned the timber would be very valuable. When Rasputin returned from Tsarskoe he repeated his conversation [with the Emperor]. Nicholas had said there would be no advance. . . . "But when will you advance?" asked Rasputin. "We shall have the rifles only in two months; before that I cannot. . . ."

It is easy to see all the advantage which Berlin would be able to obtain from this valuable piece of information.

This brings us to the tragic end of Lord Kitchener when the *Hampshire* was lost. In the letter of Alexandra of May 22 (which corresponds to June 5 of the Gregorian calendar) there is the postscript:

"One says that Kitchener on the 28th is due to arrive here or at Headquarters."

---

[5] Here Chwostoff mentioned the name of one of the shady financiers with whom Rasputin was very friendly.

Again Rasputin

One shudders at the thought that this "one says" means loose talk by Rasputin in the presence of enemy agents. Incidentally, the Kitchener tragedy supplies an excellent illustration of the influence of Rasputin over the mind of Alexandra. After the receipt of the news she wrote to her husband:

"Kitchener, what a tragedy! A real nightmare and what a loss for the English!"

To which Nicholas rejoined:

"My feelings yesterday were of a mixed nature; joy at our successes competed with the pain caused by the sad news about Kitchener."

Yet, about a fortnight later, Alexandra wrote:

"Our Friend believes that it is a good thing for us that Kitchener is dead, because later on he could have harmed Russia. And there is no harm in the fact that his papers were lost with him. You see, He fears the English attitude after the War when the peace negotiations will begin."

Rasputin, it cannot be denied, had definite political views. He represented the deep pacifism of the Russian people. For the legend about the combativeness of the *moujik* and of his representative the Russian soldier is only a legend. The Russian language is the only one, as far as we know, which instead of the expression "go to war," makes the soldiers say: "We are being driven to fight." In an old number of the newspaper *Novoye Vremia* (1913, No. 13266) we find mentioned the words Rasputin used when speaking to a journalist about the horrors of war:

Christians prepare for war, preach war, torture themselves and torture all others. War is a bad thing, and yet Christians, instead of humbling themselves, go straight towards it. . . . Generally speaking there is no use in war, in depriving each other of life and of the good things of life, in breaking the law of Christ and murdering the soul before the predestined time. What is the use to me if I defeat and conquer you: I will have to guard and fear you and always you will be against me. This comes from the sword. But I can always conquer you with Christian love and I fear nought. Let the German, Turks fight each other—that is their misfortune and blindness. They will not find anything and only will hasten their own destruction. But we in love and quietness we shall overcome all others.

Here are the makings of a philosophy which breeds conscientious objectors. It would be curious to study the points of contact between Tolstoy and Rasputin, who, both of them, are the products of a national soul, full of contradictions and subject to a swift change of shade and light. Rasputin was evil! Yes, in the light of the facts before us, we say that he was evil. But evil in him was congenital and lay lightly upon him. Out of the thickness of the popular mass he came backed by inchoate, but powerful, spiritual elements. He completed the destruction of the State and some day Russians will be found, who, with their traditional fatalism, will say that Rasputin had a historical mission to fulfil. But this issue does not concern us at present. What we have to establish is that, when the Great War broke out, Russia had for an Emperor—Nicholas II—an uxorious man with a weak will. He was dominated by the Empress—Alexandra—a woman who had become a neurasthenic and a visionary. She was the obedient follower of Rasputin, a sketch of whose personality we have attempted to give above. Russia was not able to stand the strain of the great struggle until the end. Knowing what we know we are surprised that she withstood disruption for as long as she did.

CHAPTER XV

FAMILY LIFE

"O the pure all is pure." The irony contained in this German proverb makes it no less true. The fact must not surprise us, therefore, that the single-minded nobility of Alexandra made her blind to the sordidness in the nature of Rasputin. She passed by unseeing, and to her the friendship with this man was a beautiful and holy thing. Slanderous rumours, coupling her name with that of the "Man of God," had reached the Empress. They made her angry, but failed to impress her. The letters she wrote to Nicholas during the War mention that Rasputin had ceased to come to the Palace in the Emperor's absence. A woman with an uneasy conscience would have explained: "Henceforward I shall see Grigory only before witnesses." Or even she would have declared: "People are wicked and I must give up seeing Grigory altogether." But the thought of giving up the precious friendship does not occur to Alexandra. Secure in the castle of her virtue she tells Nicholas: "I cannot have our Friend come to the Palace, because of the rumours." She then serenely relates the interview she has just had in the privacy of the house of Anna Virubova.

Family Life

As the years went by Nicholas and his wife raised ever higher the wall which protected their private life from the eyes, not only of the public, but even of their relatives. Apart from their letters and diaries, which we now possess, there are therefore few reliable records to throw light on the subject. Of these the best—it stands unique—is the story of thirteen years passed at the Imperial Court by Pierre Gilliard, the Swiss tutor of the unfortunate boy Alexis.[1] But even Gilliard, who lived in daily touch with the family, is obliged to confess that his knowledge is not perfect. About Rasputin he has not much to say. Perhaps he does not want to say all he knows on this distasteful subject. His evidence—what there is of it—is however conclusive:

The first at Court to attempt to show up the impostor was Mademoiselle Tioutchova, the governess of the Grand Duchesses. Her efforts were broken against the blind faith of the Tsarina. Among the charges she made against Rasputin were several, which in her indignation, she had not checked with sufficient care, so that their falsity was absolutely patent to her sovereign. Realizing her impotence and with a view to discharging her responsibilities, she asked that, in any case, Rasputin should not be allowed on the floor occupied by the children.[2] The Tsar then intervened and Her Majesty yielded, not because her faith was shaken, but merely for the sake of peace. . . . Al-

---

[1] *Thirteen Years at the Russian Court*, Pierre Gilliard.
[2] Rodzianko, the President of the Duma, says in his memoirs: "It became known that he (Rasputin) had seduced the nurse of the Imperial children."

though I was then no more than one of the Grand
Duchesses' professors—it was during the winter of
1910—Mademoiselle Tioutchova herself told me all
about this debate and its vicissitudes. But I confess
that all that time I was still far from accepting all
the extraordinary stories about Rasputin. Relations
between the Tsarina and Mademoiselle Tioutchova
were never again what they had been, and the latter
resigned her post in the spring of 1912.

Here is the confirmation of the fact that Rasputin
was a familiar of the household to such an extent
that the governess thought it her duty to preserve her
charges from contact with him. The faith of the
Empress was not to be shaken, but in the interest of
Rasputin himself, "who, she believed, was blinded by
his very zeal and devotion," she agreed that his visits
should become more discreet. The thing which really
mattered was that he should be always at hand to
guard the boy and to give wise advice. The house
of Anna Virubova, nestling near the gates of the
Palace, became the place where the Empress met the
"Man of God." The latter, nevertheless, was not
excluded from the Palace itself and we have the direct
evidence of Gilliard that, to his knowledge, Rasputin
came several times to the rooms of Alexis. But Gilliard confesses that he was kept in the dark about
many things. Referring to the year 1913, he says:

At that time I still knew very little about the
staretz [3] and I was searching everywhere for material

---

[3] Staretz, literally: old man, is the name often given in Russia
to men leading a holy life.

on which to base my judgment, for his personality interested me decidedly. But it was anything but easy. The children never mentioned Rasputin's name, and in my presence even avoided the slightest allusion to his existence. I realized that in so doing they were acting on their mother's instructions. The Tsarina, no doubt, feared that as a foreigner and not Orthodox, I was incapable of understanding the nature of the feelings of herself and her family towards the *staretz,* feelings, which made them revere him as a saint. By imposing this duty of silence on my pupils she allowed me to ignore Rasputin, or conveyed to me her desire that I should behave as if I knew nothing about him. She thus deprived me of any chance of taking sides against a man, whose very name I realized I did not know.

Gilliard adds: "the children saw Rasputin, when he was with their parents." We gain thus a clear perception of the standing of the "Man of God": he remains on intimate terms with the whole family; husband, wife and children "revere him as a saint." This should be sufficient to disprove the slanders about the moral turpitude of the Empress. Hysterical, unbalanced, mad perhaps to a certain point—she was all that, but her purity is above suspicion. Otherwise she could not have remained until the end the pivot of a touching family life. Her husband worshipped her and the children clustered around her with an energy of love which is the sign of a closely knit existence. Alexandra was the mother—the chief of the family—for Nicholas, adoring her as he did and engrossed with affairs of State, gladly left the parental authority in her keeping. Gilliard testifies that she carried out her maternal obligations with devotion and a deep sense of duty. But her health was indifferent and often the preoccupation with political events made her appear absent-minded. On the historical day when Nicholas was forced by the clearly expressed will of the nation to agree to the convocation of the Duma—the legislative assembly (this was in October, 1905)—Alexandra was present as usual at the lesson given by Gilliard to the two eldest grand duchesses, Olga and Tatyana.

In spite of all she could do [says Gilliard], her face betrayed her inward agitation. She made obvious efforts to concentrate her thoughts upon us, but soon relapsed into a melancholy reverie, in which she was utterly lost. Her work slipped from her fingers to her lap. Age had clasped her hands, and her gaze, following her thoughts, seemed lost and indifferent to the things about her. I had made a practice, when the lesson was over, of shutting my book and waiting until the Tsarina rose as a signal for me to retire. This time, notwithstanding the silence, which followed the end of the lesson, she was so lost in thought that she did not move. The minutes passed and the children fidgeted. I opened my book again and went on reading. Not for a quarter of an hour, when one of the Grand Duchesses went up to her mother, did she realize the time.

At the moment Gilliard did not know that Alexandra was full of anguish at the thought that her husband was placed in the terrible necessity of breaking the pact with heaven concluded at his coronation and to which she attached such importance. He found another and no less plausible explanation:

The Tsarina's health, already tried by her anxiety about the menace hanging over the Tsarevitch's head, by degrees prevented her from following her daughters' education. At the time I did not realize what was the cause of her apparent indifference, and was inclined to censure her for it, but it was not long before events showed me my mistake. [This sentence refers to the discovery by Gilliard of the secret of the tragic disease by which the boy Alexis was afflicted.] The Tsarina was still a beautiful woman at that time. She was tall and slender, and carried herself superbly. But all this ceased to count the moment one looked into her eyes—those speaking, grey-blues, which mirrored the emotions of a sensitive soul.

The same eyes looked out of the face of her unfortunate son:

I saw the Tsarevitch, Alexis Nicolayevitch, then a baby of eighteen months old, for the first time under the following circumstances. As usual, I had gone that day to the Palace, where my duties called me several times a week. I was just finishing my lesson with Olga Nicolayevna, when the Tsarina entered the room, carrying the son and heir. She came towards us, and evidently wished to show the one member of the family I did not yet know. I could see she was transfused by the delirious joy of a mother, who at last has seen her dearest wish fulfilled. She was proud and happy in the beauty of the child. The Tsarevitch was certainly one of the handsomest babies one could imagine with his lovely fair curls and his great blue-grey eyes under their fringe of long curling lashes. He had the fresh pink colour of a healthy child and, when he smiled there were two little dimples in his chubby cheeks. . . . At the first meeting I saw the Tsarina press the little boy to her with the convulsive movement of a mother, who always seems in fear of her child's life. Yet with her the caress and the look which accompanied it revealed a secret apprehension so marked and poignant that I was struck at once. I had not very long to wait to know its meaning.

His book establishes Gilliard in the position of a reliable witness on the family life of the last Romanoff Emperor. The work of this honest Republican is free from Russian prejudices and preconceived notions and must be read by those, who wish to study the life of Alexandra.

Let us look at the family life of Nicholas and Alexandra in 1914, just before the outbreak of the Great War. Twenty years of married life have had a sobering influence on passion, but wedded love shines with a warm light. The private apartments in the great Palace of Tsarskoe Selo shelter a union, the joys of which political adversity and family misfortune only serve to make more precious.

"Heavy trials everywhere, but at home, in our nest bright sunshine," writes the Empress, and her husband, whose mind is attuned to hers, says in his letter on the same day: "With a deeply loving heart and on my knees I thank you for your love, attachment, friendship and patience, which you have shown through these long years of our married life." The word "long" is used to express the pride of a faithful and happy lover. How could it be otherwise, if among her most valued possessions Alexandra counts the dress she wore on the day of her betrothal and the modest brooch, which Nicholas bought for her in a shop in Cowes, when he came to visit Queen Victoria in 1894?

"Ever, Nicky, my own, your very own deeply loving old wifey Alix" and "Very tenderest, fondest kisses from your very own old wifey Sunny," so conclude letters addressed to "My very own beloved One" and to "My own beloved Darling." The faith of the Empress in the statesmanlike abilities of Nicholas has suffered, but the love of Sunny for Nicky endures and has become more poignant, because it is pervaded by a sense of protecting motherliness. Women love heroes passionately and ordinary men faithfully, especially if harmony exists between the sexes.

The Empress is a beautiful woman still. She is tall and slender and her carriage is suberb. The eyes —the mirror of a sensitive soul—attract and compel attention. At unguarded moments there is a look in them indicating mental strain. The perfect lines of the mouth are marred by a tightening of the lips—the result of the battle against emotions, which threaten to upset a painfully maintained self-control. The general health is shaky. The heart is enlarged and physical effort has become a burden. Alexandra finds it difficult to go up one flight of stairs from her rooms to the floor occupied by the children. The long walks with Nicholas have been discontinued. A wheeled chair is often brought into use, when the husband wants to take his wife out for an airing in the park. In addition to other infirmities the Empress suffers from excruciating neuralgia of the face caused by a decayed tooth, which out of coquetry she refuses to have removed. The settee in the Mauve Room has become the place where she is usually to be found, half recumbent with her needlework or with the writing pad on her knees. In this position she remains for hours at a stretch, often, in the desire for solitude, sending away even her husband and the children, who come to keep her company.

But weakness and melancholy disappear as if by enchantment, when any one of the family is ill, especially when the boy has his attacks of bleeding. The Empress runs up and down the stairs with the agility of a young girl, she instals herself near the bed of the patient, ministering to every want with vigilant and loving solicitude, and remains whole nights without sleep. When the critical moment is past a reaction sets in: the Empress lies on the couch, pale, incapable of movement, taking little interest in her surroundings. After each alarm she is stricken with an immense lassitude, more mental than physical. But her strong will battles against the depression and she begins taking again an interest in the life of her

family, especially in the troubles which ceaselessly
assail her beloved husband.

After twenty years the Emperor has not changed
much physically. His bearing is alert and the muscu-
lar force, unsuspected in the slight body, has been preserved. He is a strong walker and an indefatigable
rower and tennis player. The power of enjoying life
has not been lost: the Emperor romps with the children like a schoolboy and is ready to get up at an
unearthly hour to stalk the elusive capercailye. But
the fine eyes, inherited from his mother, reflect at
times the strained expression, which so often dwells
in those of the Empress. Nicholas during his reign
had had his share of bad fortune; with a shrug of the
shoulders he confesses his belief that he was born
under an unlucky star. Time has not added to the
intellectual powers of the Emperor, yet it has given
to him at least a technical knowledge of the affairs
of Government, which stands him in good stead in the
routine work of autocracy. Day in, day out, he plod-
dingly performs what he considers to be his duty. He
feels that the rift between him and the nation is becoming wider, but he is convinced that Providence is
watching over his throne and that things will come
out right in the end, if not for himself, then for his
son.

This son is the apple of the eye of the parents.
They watch over him with unceasing anxiety, for they
know that at any moment a fatal accident may deprive
them of their treasure. The boy is in his tenth year

and an extremely handsome child. The long, finely
chiselled face, the delicate features and the auburn hair
with a copper glint in it are like those of the mother.
But where the likeness becomes positively uncanny is
in the large blue-grey eyes, at the moments, especially,
when during an attack of bleeding, there comes into
them a look of tragic surprise. A solid spiritual link
exists between mother and son; they do not need
words to understand one another. Their relations are
permeated with a charming tenderness. At bedtime
Alexandra comes to her son's cot and, nestling in her
arms, he says his prayers and then promptly turns off
the light over his head:

"Mummy, you are my light. The room is dark
when you go."

The Countess Kleinmichel, the aristocratic lady who
lived under three reigns, has given us in her memoirs
a poignant little picture.[4] At a gay children's party
at one of the Grand Ducal palaces she saw Alexandra:

"She sat with the Tsarevitch in her lap, silent, sad
and listlessly indifferent to her surroundings. From
time to time she petted her son, restraining his viva-
ciousness. She suddenly got up and said to the Emperor: 'Nicky, it is time to go.'"

Alexis would like to join the other children in their
noisy games, but he is not allowed to do so for fear
of a fall or some kick which would start the fatal
bleeding. Two male nurses—sturdy sailors from the
Imperial yacht—are attached to his person and watch

---

[4] M. Kleinmichel, *Is Potonuvshago Mira*, Berlin, 1923.

over him day and night. Gilliard, who has just taken over the duties of tutor, is appalled by the results of this constant supervision, which makes the child so dependent on others and hinders the development of his self-reliance. A physically delicate child is being turned into an individual without character, not to speak of the fact that the constant control is humiliating and tends to develop in the boy deceitfulness and cunning. Here occurs an incident which throws light on the character of Alexandra.

M. Gilliard, as we have said, believed in the necessity of making the child more independent. He pointed out to the Empress that it would be better to let Alexis have more freedom so that he should become accustomed to find in himself the energy to control his own motion, this being the best guarantee against future accidents. Here the strong will of Alexandra asserted itself. She agreed with the tutor's arguments and decided to risk the experiment of relieving Alexis of the presence of his guardians. She was aware of the additional risk, which was thereby incurred, but in her love she found the strength to repress her anxiety. The change proved itself beneficial. The boy was delighted and became less capricious and more amenable to the influence of those who were in charge of his education. But then a slight accident happened: Alexis slipped in the schoolroom and knocked his knee against the leg of a table. The next day he could not walk and the day after that the internal haemorrhage had extended from the knee down the leg. The child was suffering intense pain from the pressure of the extravasated blood on the nerves and the danger of blood-poisoning grew worse every hour. Alexandra accepted the responsibility without flinching. She did not utter a word of reproach. On the contrary, she gave M. Gilliard to understand that she did not hold him responsible for what had happened and with a "truly touching" kindness she consoled him, associating with him in the vigil at the bedside of the little sufferer.

The Tsarevitch lay in bed groaning piteously. His head rested on his mother's arm and his small, deathly white face was unrecognizable. At times the groans ceased and he murmured the one word, Mummy, in which he expressed all his sufferings and distress. His mother kissed him on the hair, forehead and eyes, as if the touch of her lips could have relieved the pain and restored some of the life which was leaving him. Think of the tortures of that mother. . . . Now I understood the secret tragedy of her life.

In these circumstances the education of the boy could not be satisfactory. After every attack weeks and even months passed before the regular course of study could be resumed. Alexis was not stupid, but he had no inclination to acquire knowledge and, in the absence of competition with children of his age, which might have stimulated his zeal, his progress was both slow and fragmentary. In his intervals of health he was of a cheerful disposition and showed no signs of an overbearing nature, which the knowledge of his exalted position could easily have engendered. He was always displeased, when, according to the ancient custom, peasants who approached him knelt or tried to kiss his hand. Alexis felt his isolation keenly and his tutor was anxious to provide for him the company of boys of his age. It is characteristic of relations in the Imperial family that the children of the grand dukes were not encouraged to associate with the heir to the throne. Neither did he have any friends among the sons of the nobility. He was allowed to play sometimes with the two sons of his doctor, but his favourite was Titi, a little fellow several years his junior, the son of Mme. Dehn, the wife of a naval officer to whom the Empress had taken a great liking.

An interesting glimpse of the boy is given us by Rodzianko, the President of the Duma. He relates in his memoirs [5] that on one occasion, before the War, when he had been received in audience by the Emperor, the latter sent for his son.

I introduced myself as the biggest and fattest man in Russia [Rodzianko was inordinately tall and fat] at which the boy broke out into a merry laugh. On my asking him whether yesterday's collection on behalf of an "Ear of Corn" [a flagday in favour of a charity] had been successful, the child's singularly attractive face lit up with pleasure, as he answered quickly: "Oh yes, I collected fifty roubles. That is a lot, you know." . . . As I left the room I heard the Tsarevitch's loud whisper: "Who's that?" and the Tsar's answer: "The President of the Duma." The little Tsarevitch ran after me into the hall, and all the time

[5] M. Rodzianko, *The Reign of Rasputin.*

stood peeping at me through the glass door. . . . The smiling Derevenko [a sailor attached to Alexis] appeared on the scene. I scrutinized the faces of the footmen, soldiers and Cossacks standing at attention in the hall. How lovingly they all looked at the Tsarevitch.

The Emperor was proud of his son and, thinking of the future, tried to keep him as much as possible in the public eye. At military reviews, religious ceremonies and other public functions the boy appeared next to his father. Unfortunately, sometimes he had to be carried because of his weak leg. When Nicholas became Commander-in-Chief during the War and was obliged to remain for months at a time far from home Alexandra sacrificed her own feelings to what she believed to be the best interests of Alexis and let him go to stay with his father at Headquarters. She could never become accustomed to the idea that her son would not live, or that his health would never allow him to reign. On the contrary her thoughts were always concentrated on his future. She believed that he had inherited from her the strong will she missed in Nicholas and she fondly hoped that it would be given to Alexis to retrieve some day the glories of autocracy sadly damaged by the concessions which Nicholas had been obliged to make to the popular demand. The Empress believed that Alexis, given to her by heaven through the intercession of St. Seraphim as the crowning joy of her marriage and the fulfilment of the destinies of the dynasty, was under the special

protection of divine Providence, which would protect
him from all harm and lead him to a great and glorious
destiny. She made no secret therefore of her prefer-
ence for the boy, to whom his sisters were expected to
concede the first place in the affection of the parents.

The Grand Duchess Olga, the eldest daughter of
Nicholas and Alexandra, in the year before the War
was eighteen and her sister Tatyana, sixteen. To distinguish them from their younger sisters: Marie, born
in 1899, and Anastasia, born in 1901, the two girls
were known in the family as the "big pair." The
daughters had not inherited their mother's remarkable
beauty. Tatyana was the only one, who with her supple figure, fine features and expressive eyes, attracted
attention. The others were a throwback to the sturdy,
broad-faced type of their grandfather Alexander III.
All four more than compensated what they may have
lacked in good looks by their air of splendid health
and their buoyant spirits. The contrast between their
glorious youth and the delicate constitution of the only
son was sometimes painful to behold and constantly
reminded Alexandra of the tragic secret of her family
life.

Death came swiftly to these young creatures and
we cannot tell if they would have been, if they had
lived, remarkable in any way in their maturity. With
the exception of Olga, who as a child possessed a remarkably quick brain, the sisters were not intellectually
brilliant. They were attentive and even painstaking
pupils, but knowledge possessed for them no particular

attraction and as they grew up their progress became even less noticeable. Even Olga, as her teachers had the occasion to remark, lost some of her original mental agility. This may be explained by the extremely secluded life led by the family. There were no girl friends, no social entertainments worth mentioning, very few amusements and practically no contact with the world outside a very restricted family circle. Olga and Tatyana, at the time we are considering, had not been yet to a real ball. Alexandra, shunning the world herself, forgot that this cloistered régime was deadly for her children. The girls accepted the mode of life prescribed for them without complaint. This, perhaps, because they knew none better. But, when one thinks of it, these grand duchesses, the daughters of a powerful monarch, were satisfied with a life which would drive any modern girl to despair and revolt. Until the end even Olga did not have a room which she could call her own, and all her movements were closely watched by her mother. Alexandra, no doubt, wanted to do the right thing by her daughters and at times was assailed by doubts as to their future. The question of marriage, as in all royal families, arose early and from time to time Nicholas and Alexandra discussed it between themselves. While German princesses, when they married into the Russian Imperial family, were expected to join the Orthodox Church, a change of religion by Russian grand duchesses at their marriage had always been viewed with disfavour. When the daughter of an Emperor married a foreign prince the right was reserved for her to remain in her old faith. This was the case of Grand Duchess Marie, the daughter of Alexander II, who became the wife of Alfred, the son of Queen Victoria and Duke of Saxe-Coburg-Gotha. She had her own private chapel and Orthodox priest at Gotha, as is mentioned in the diary of Nicholas. Alexander III disliked so much the idea of Russian grand duchesses marrying foreigners that for both his daughters husbands were found in the Imperial family itself. Nicholas and Alexandra had planned to marry their eldest child to a young cousin, the Grand Duke Dímitry, who at one time had been a favourite with them. Olga apparently was inclined to favour the suit of the handsome and brilliant young man, but Alexandra learnt details of his gay life as a bachelor of which she did not approve and the project was dropped. Another grand duke, whose candidature was strongly pressed by his mother, she refused to consider at all because of his morals.

Alexandra refers to this incident in her letter of January 28, 1916:

> . . . and your tender caresses, oh how deeply I thank you for them. They warmed me. . . . Oh could but our children be equally blessed in their married lives. The idea of Boris is too unsympathetic and the child would, I feel convinced, never agree to marry him and I should perfectly well understand her. Only never let Miechen (Grand Duchess Marie Pavlovna) guess that other thoughts have filled the child's head and heart. Those are a young girl's holy secrets which

others must not know of. It would terribly hurt
Olga, who is susceptible.

Foreign princes offered themselves in numbers, but
the Grand Duchess was so imbued with the Russian
spirit that the idea of living abroad frightened her.
For political reasons Nicholas was not averse to giving
his daughter to Prince Carol, the prospective heir to
the Roumanian throne.[6]

An alliance with Roumania would have been to the
advantage of the Russian plans for aggrandizement in
the basin of the Black Sea and for the ultimate conquest of Constantinople. The marriage was also attractive because the Royal House of Roumania is Orthodox. A visit in State was arranged and Nicholas,
Alexandra and their daughters were given a splendid
reception when they arrived at the Roumanian port of
Constantza. But Olga had been promised by her
parents that they would not force her to marry against
her will. She disliked Carol and therefore nothing
came of the plan. In a letter to Nicholas, Alexandra,
commenting upon the visit of a young officer, one of
the few known to her personally, says:

"My little M. came for an hour yesterday evening
after dinner at Ania's. We had not seen him for one
and a half years. Looks flourishing, more of a man
now, an adorable boy still, a perfect son-in-law he
would have been. Why are foreign princes not as
nice?" (March 17, 1916.)

---

[6] This is the Prince Carol who later was disinherited for his
marital adventures and dissolute life.

Family Life

One of the reasons why Olga had many suitors was that she was a great heiress. By the will of Alexander III, who fondly hoped that the first child of Nicholas would be a boy, his private fortune, running into millions, was left to the eldest grandchild. The Grand Duchess herself was probably ignorant of the fact. She certainly was kept very short of money indeed. Alexandra did not encourage the spending of money. As a young girl she had had a meagre pocket allowance and had acquired parsimonious habits, which fitted in with an inherited inclination for hoarding. The only luxury in which the grand duchesses were allowed to indulge, was, as far as we can discover, the use of perfume in their bath, while their mother remained faithful to ordinary unscented soap. If any of the girls had suggested the provision of a manicuring set she would have been called a profligate. But they did not ask for any such sort of refined thing.

It was an exciting, unforgettable day in the monotonous existence of the two elder girls, when their father appointed each of them Honorary Chief of a cavalry regiment. The "Chiefs" received deputations from "their" officers and men and were allowed, dressed in regimentals over their riding skirts, to accompany the Emperor on horseback during a military review. When the War broke out, work in hospital became an absorbing interest and a great distraction. Carrying out the duties of ordinary nurses the grand duchesses had the opportunity of coming into contact with a large number of people. Later their mother allowed them to become members of the committees of charitable institutions, thus giving them a chance of becoming acquainted with administrative work. Curiously enough it was in connexion with this committee work that the Grand Duchess Olga obtained the first impression that something was wrong with the relations between the throne and society. In a letter of Alexandra to Nicholas we find the following remark:

"Olga had a Committee yesterday evening, but it did not last long. Volodia Volch,[7] who always has a smile or two for her, avoided her eyes and never once smiled. You see how our girlies have learned to watch people and their faces. They have developed much interiorly through all this suffering. They know all we go through, is necessary and ripens them. They are happily at times great babies, but have the insight and the feelings of the soul of much wiser things. As our Friend says: they have passed heavy 'kursy.' "[8] (December 16, 1916.)

Thus again we cross the trail of Rasputin. That the reference to his view on the grand duchesses is not casual and that the Empress often talked to him of her family is proved by the following extract:

"Our Friend is so contented with our girlies, says they have gone through heavy 'kursy' for their age and their souls have much developed. They are really great dears and no nice now with Ania. They have

---

[7] Diminutive for Prince Vladimir Volonsky, Vice-Minister for the Interior.

[8] "Kursy"—Russian for a course of learning.

shared all our emotions and it has taught them to see people with open eyes, so that it will be a great help to them later in life." (December 6, 1916.)

The reference to Anna Virubova is significant. Clearly the girls were not quite as friendly with this messenger of Rasputin as the Empress would have wished. But gradually they were won over. In the letters of Alexandra there are many references to visits paid by her in the company of her daughters to the house of Anna Virubova, where "our Friend" met them, talked to them about religion and was consulted as an oracle on all possible questions. Mme. Dehn, whose evidence we have no reason to suspect, because she was not unfriendly to Rasputin, says in her memoirs that the family saw him at the Palace at least once a month.

But these extracts show also how close was the association between parents and children. Nicholas talked freely in the presence of the latter about his troubles and discussed with Alexandra the measures he intended to take and the appointments to be made. There is no doubt about it; they were a united family. The children had been brought up by Alexandra in a feeling of respect, of reverence even, for their father, the Emperor. Their mother they adored and her word to them was law. They watched over her tenderly and, when she was unwell, arranged that one of them should be always near her. An interest which all the members of the family had in common was photography; they were snapshotting each other and other people all the time and much time was given to the pasting of the photographs into special albums. Nicholas loved reading aloud; between dinner and bedtime the family assembled around the couch on which Alexandra reclined working at her embroidery, while Nicholas read to them some interesting novel. But it does not appear that his choice of literature was particularly good. From the diary which he kept during his imprisonment we learn, with some surprise, that he read *Peace and War* of Tolstoy for the first time in 1918 in Tobolsk.[9] Of sport for the children there was very little. They rowed on the large pond in the park and played a little tennis, but when at Tsarskoe they preferred the winter months, because then with the help of their father they were allowed to build for themselves a lofty snow mountain down which they tobogganed on their little sledges. They were also allowed to keep animals. The boy had a donkey, found for him with great difficulty, because Russia is not precisely the place where these animals are numerous. There were dogs of all descriptions and cats. One of the dogs, a tiny Pekinese, "Jimmy," went later with the family to prison and his bones were found in the mineshaft down which the ashes of the burnt bodies of the family had been flung by the assassins.

---

[9] The diary also shows that the last book read by Nicholas, already in Yekaterinenburg, where he was murdered, was *Paul I* by Mereshkowsky. He notes in the diary that the tragic end of his ancestor—Paul I was strangled by his officers—produced on him a deep impression.

Family Life

The family always looked forward to the time when in the hottest weeks of the northern summer they would embark in their fine yacht the *Standard* for a cruise among skerries of the Finnish Gulf. The thousands of islands, islets and rocks, which form a belt along the coast of Finland, open sometimes, forming a lakelike expanse, protected from the swell of the open sea. In some such secluded spot, the *Standard* would let drop its anchor, while torpedo-boats watched all around in the passes to prevent the intrusion of unasked stranger upon the privacy of the Emperor. The greatest pleasure of Nicholas was to row his wife about in a small boat, or to explore the labyrinth of the skerries in a launch, or to disembark upon some island for a day with the guns, or to have a family picnic on the sandy shore of a sheltered cove. Nicholas and Alexandra treated the officers and men of the yacht as their personal friends. The sailors of the Guard, who formed the crew, were a picked body of men and their attachment to the Imperial family was believed to be as solid as a rock. During the Revolution Alexandra's most bitter disappointment was to see the sailors deserting the Palace. The officers of the *Standard* were envied in the service, because of the possibility afforded them to approach the Emperor daily in conditions which favoured intimacy. For some of them this was the beginning of a splendid career and for most it meant a shower of favours in one form or another. Among them was "N. P." who was treated by Nicholas and Alexandra as a dear friend. In the letters of Alexandra, which we possess, he is mentioned one hundred and ninety-two times. As far as we know he was the only person who could call the "Man of God" "Rasputin" in her presence without receiving more than a gentle rebuke. "N. P.'s" memoirs, if published, will have an historical value and would be invaluable for the rehabilitation of the name of a much maligned Empress.

In the spring the Emperor and his family usually went to stay in the Crimea to enjoy its warm and equable climate, while Tsarskoe Selo was made uncomfortable by rain and mist. A new palace had been built for their use according to plans prepared under the supervision of Nicholas and Alexandra. It was replete with modern comfort, but in its appointments and furnishing it also showed their lack of artistic feeling. But this was a failing hereditary in the Romanoff family. Their lack of taste, particularly in the question of internal decorations was proverbial.

CHAPTER XVI

THE EMPRESS RULES

OR years Europe had been arming. The Germans, when they signed the Treaty of Peace, admitted that the catastrophe, in which the Continent had been involved, had "originated in the declaration of war by Austria-Hungary against Serbia and by Germany against Russia and France and in the invasion of Belgium." [1] Thus from a formal point of view the guilt of Germany was established. In fact it was confirmed by the German attack on little neutral Belgium. But, in reality, the whole of Europe must be held responsible for the conflict, which all clearly foresaw, for which all feverishly prepared and which none found the courage to denounce openly. The professional soldiers, as was their duty, armed for the clash, while politicians and diplomats lost valuable time in the pettifoggery of secret intrigues. If governments had understood that war is too serious an enterprise to be left in the hands of the militarists, there would probably have been no war, for public opinion would have been warned and the democratic checks—the best instrument for peace—could have been brought into action.

---

[1] Preamble to the Treaty of Versailles.

But those who knew were paralyzed by the preconceived notion that war could not be avoided. They prepared for it, not against it. The criminal conspiracy of silence was so great that in all countries the public was taken by surprise.

Nicholas personally was for peace. He had burned his fingers in the war against Japan, caused by his desire of aggrandizement. The revolutionary movement, which came after, forcing him to make concessions to the national demand for a constitution, had shown him the danger to the dynasty of taking part in a new warlike adventure. The historical material available proves that at the critical moment Nicholas wavered and delayed and that the order for the general mobilization was extracted from him by the combined effort of his Minister for Foreign Affairs and of his Chief of the General Staff, who, conscious of the danger of being outstripped by the Germans, pressed for a decision. At last Sazonoff, the Foreign Minister, obtained the fateful order, passed it on immediately to General Janushkewitch, telling him, "to tear off the telephone wire," evidently, in the fear that Nicholas would change his mind after all. It is Gilliard who tells us the true reason for the Emperor's hesitation:

While tempers were rising and the diplomats were setting the machinery of all the chancelleries in motion, heartrending telegrams left for distant Siberia, where Rasputin was slowly recovering from his wound at Tioumen. They were nearly all of the same tenor:

"We are horrified at the prospect of war. Do you think it possible? Pray for us. Help us with your counsel." Rasputin would reply that war must be avoided at any cost if the worst calamities were not to overtake the dynasty and the Empire. [In the winter of 1918, when I was at Tioumen, I saw the copies of these very telegrams. Later on I found it impossible to get hold of the text again.] This advice was consonant with the dearest wish of the Tsar, whose pacific intentions could not be doubted for a moment. We had only to see him during that terrible last week to realize what mental and moral torture he had passed through.

Rasputin, who, as we have shown, was a convinced pacifist and who shrewdly suspected the danger to the monarchy, had been for peace at any price. During the Balkan crisis of 1912 his advice had been against military adventures of any kind. Had he been in St. Petersburg during these fateful weeks, who knows if he would not have made it even more difficult for Nicholas to decide to accept the challenge of Germany? But Rasputin was away. He had gone to his native village to attend to his personal affairs and had been stabbed dangerously in the abdomen by a young woman whom he had seduced. Fears had been entertained for his life, and he had been rushed off to the hospital in the town of Tioumen near by, where a surgeon sent by special train from St. Petersburg operated upon him. Rasputin's convalescence was swift, but he was still in a hospital when the war broke out. Alexandra, accustomed to consult her friend on all important questions, felt his absence during the critical days in the summer of 1914 as a visitation from heaven.

Then a remarkable change occurred in Nicholas. The Russian nation, although taken by surprise by the war news, accepted it in the spirit of a patriotic exaltation, not doubting for a moment that Germany, which had overrun helpless Belgium, and Austria-Hungary, which had insulted the much smaller Serbia, were criminal disturbers of the peace of Europe. Suddenly, Nicholas, who for years had seen a chasm opening between himself and his subjects, found himself carried upwards on a wave of popularity and devotion. Internal politics were forgotten for the moment and the nation acclaimed the Emperor as its leader in a great and just cause.

Gilliard, who obtained these details from one of the daughters, says that on the evening when war was declared the family waited long for Nicholas to come to dinner. The Empress had just told one of the grand duchesses to call her father, when the latter appeared, looking very pale, and in a voice which he tried to keep calm, told them what had happened. On learning the news Alexandra began to weep and her daughters, likewise, seeing their mother's distress shed tears. The family had attended evensong in the Palace church, and it was remarked that Nicholas wore an air of exhaustion. The pouches which appeared under his eyes when he was agitated were in evidence. He was praying with all the fer-

Empress Alexandra Feodorovna at the Time of the Great War

vour of his nature. At his side was Alexandra on whose careworn face was "that look of suffering I had so often seen at her son's bedside." She prayed fervently, as if she wished to banish an evil dream. . . .

On the next day the Emperor went to St. Petersburg. The streets were filled with an excited throng which acclaimed him, waving flags and singing the national anthem. The great square in front of the Winter Palace was black with a closely packed crowd. The Emperor was in the Palace speaking to the chiefs of his army and receiving the diplomatic corps. In the throne room he read out to a highly strung audience the manifesto, in which he acquainted Russia with his decision to resist the unfair demands of Germany by the force of arms, as all attempts to maintain the peace had come to naught. He then came out on the balcony which overlooks the great square. He stood there quite alone, his diminutive figure silhouetted against the reddish wall. The crowd knelt as one man and sang the anthem with enthusiasm, conveying to the Emperor the conviction that the nation was at one with him in this matter of life and death. The author, who had received the order to leave for the front on the next morning, was in the square at this moment and can certify that the atmosphere was one of great enthusiasm, while a current of sympathy seemed to have established itself between the thousands of people and the little figure high up on the balcony. Processions, carrying flags and

singing patriotic songs, moved afterwards through the
streets of the capital, meetings were held in front of
the allied embassies and the representatives of Great
Britain, France, Belgium and Serbia were acclaimed
with frenzied cheers, when they appeared. A number of rowdies unfortunately slipped through the
police cordon and invaded the building of the German
embassy—built after the plans of William II himself
—now empty of its diplomatic occupants. Enthusiastic fellows climbing to the roof precipitated from the
latter the two bronze giants, which for so long had
insulted the good taste of the Russians by their crude
nudity. They fell with a dull crash on to the Ambassador's mattresses which had been thrown out on
the pavement just before.

The events through which they were passing broke
through the reserve maintained by Nicholas and Alexandra. Gilliard, who was so intimately associated
with their family troubles and anxieties, confesses in
his diary that the Imperial couple never discussed
political or personal questions with him. But now the
conventional barriers of etiquette had fallen. Nicholas
spoke with confidence and frankness of his absolute
faith in the future:

"Speaking personally, I have done everything in my
power to avert this war, and I am ready to make concessions consistent with our dignity and national honour. You cannot imagine how glad I am that all this
uncertainty is over, for I have never been through so
terrible a time as the days preceding the outbreak of

war. I am sure that there will now be a national up-
rising in Russia. . . ."

Alexandra was in a state of indignation at the news
that William II had forbidden the Dowager Empress
to continue her journey to Russia and after a period
of undignified detention had had her sent to Denmark.
She lamented:

> Fancy a monarch arresting an Empress. How
> could he descend to that? He has absolutely
> changed since the militarist party, who hate Rus-
> sia, have gained the upper hand with him. But
> I am sure he has been won over to the war against
> his will. . . . I have never liked the Emperor
> William, if only because he is not sincere. He
> is vain and has always played the comedian. He
> was always reproaching me with doing nothing
> for Germany and has always done his best to
> separate Russia and France, though I never be-
> lieved it [the Alliance] was for the good of Rus-
> sia. He will never forgive me this war. . . . I
> myself have no news of my brother [the Grand
> Duke of Hesse]. Where is he? In Belgium or
> on the French front? I shiver to think that the
> Emperor William may avenge himself against me
> by sending him to the Russian front. . . . What
> will become of Germany? What humiliation,
> what a downfall is in store for her? And all for
> the sins of the Hohenzollerns. . . . Whatever
> has happened to the Germany of my childhood?
> I have such happy and poetic memories of my
> early years in Darmstadt and the good friends I
> had there. But on my later visits Germany
> seemed a changed country. . . . I had no com-

munity of thought or feeling with any one except the old friends of days gone by. Prussia has meant Germany's ruin . . . it will be a terrible, monstrous struggle, and humanity is about to pass through ghastly sufferings. . . .

A few days later the Emperor with his wife and children went to Moscow, where they were given an enthusiastic reception by the inhabitants. Nicholas and Alexandra glowed with delight at the thought that they had reconquered the affection of their subjects. They believed that a new page had been opened in the history of autocracy in Russia: Heaven had stood by its pact with the Czar and from now on things would go well for it ever after. Their joy was damped only by the fact that Alexis, who for a number of months had been in exceptionally good health, fell a victim to a new attack of internal bleeding in the knee and, incapable of walking, had to be carried about by a stalwart Cossack of the bodyguard. But Rasputin was well again and Alexandra relied on his presence to ward off further danger from her son.

The Russian armies went into the War with a glorious *élan*. Those who have lived through the terrible years which followed will remember with pride the first period of the War, when, after a mobilization swift beyond all expectations, the Russians marched into battle, severely defeated sometimes, but always returning to the attack with incomparable courage to carry forward their standards from victory to victory.

The Empress Rules

It was the time of the "steamroller," which helped to relieve the pressure on the Allies in the west, which crushed the Austrians and instilled fear into the Germans. Where are the legions? Where are the brave men? The sickle of death, which passed a few of us by, reaped them and they lie in unnamed graves, where they fell facing the foe, or, worse still, in the cemeteries of prison camps or in the slaughter houses of the Revolution. The soldiers of other nations have their cenotaphs, but to Russian heroes the only monument is in the memory of their comrades, who saw them fight and die. The best, the bravest—the flower of the Russian nation—were swallowed up in the first heroic period of the War; they were spared the sight of the shame which came after and which their presence might have helped to avert. For the extravagance with which the army threw its best elements into the fray is responsible to a large extent for the appalling deterioration which set in later and finally transformed millions of decent soldiers into a murderous rabble.

The army in the field was commanded by the Grand Duke Nicholas Nicholayevitch. He had many qualities which make a military leader; a grasp of general principles, an ability to survey the situation as a whole, determination and personal courage. His chief fault was the inability to distinguish military qualities in his subordinates and to select the latter independently from considerations of friendship and patronage. Generals who should have been ruthlessly set aside after the first unfavourable trial were left in responsible posts and punishment was not meted out without delay to offenders in high places. Nevertheless, taking everything into consideration, the Grand Duke, of all the members of the Imperial family, was the best suited for the post of Commander-in-Chief, for which he had prepared himself by long years of careful study. Nicholas would have liked to occupy the post himself, but he met with the resistance of his most faithful advisers, who pointed out the dynastic danger of allowing an, autocrat to shoulder the responsibility for possible defeat. Nicholas had to be content with frequent visits to the fighting fronts, visits which were viewed with disfavour by the Commander-in-Chief, who on these occasions was obliged to tear himself away from his exacting duties to accompany the Emperor. As the War dragged on the whole life of the country became more and more dominated by military requirements and General Headquarters in more ways than one began to intervene in the activities of the civil administration. The Grand Duke Nicholas, by the force of circumstances, became the most prominent personage in public life so that, without in the least desiring it, he seemed to overshadow the Emperor himself.

Alexandra had taken up from the very first day of the War the cause of the wounded. With her two elder daughters, the Grand Duchesses Olga and Tatyana, she took a course of nursing. A hospital was opened in the historic Palace of Elizabeth in Tsarskoe Selo.

The Empress Rules

The halls and drawing rooms, which had seen the splendours of the court of Catherine the Great were transformed into wards, where wounded officers and men were cared for under the direct supervision of the Empress. No service seemed too low for her and in an access of nervous energy she wore out her frail strength by taking part daily in operations and in dressing the hardest cases. Not content with this personal effort Alexandra became the active head of an organization which controlled a number of sanitary trains, field ambulances and in many other ways supplemented the activities of the military hospitals and of the Red Cross. So engrossed became the Empress in her work that she gave up the few social duties which she had consented to carry out until then. Court and society saw her no more. In the uniform of a "sister," with a white headdress covering her hair, she performed her daily task at the hospital and then passed long hours in church, praying for the success of her beloved Nicholas and of the Russian arms. The public did not take kindly to her devoted conduct. They would have preferred a more spectacular Empress, supervising the work of others and spending her time in stimulating the energy of ordinary workers by her Imperial presence. The photographs which represented the Empress and her daughters performing the tasks of ordinary nurses, sitting by the beds of serious cases and chatting with the wounded aroused mixed feelings and a growing volume of criticism. Meanwhile the Empress was happy in her self-allotted duties. And she had Rasputin to advise and encourage her.

Since 1911, when public attention had been first called to the person of Rasputin and to his mysterious influence in court circles, the news had been always given out that the "Man of God" was being kept at a distance by the Empress. Rumours to that effect were constantly being put into circulation and Anna Virubova and other self-appointed apologists of the Empress, have tried to perpetuate the legend in their memoirs. So Mlle. Virubova tries to make out that "since 1911 he [that is, Rasputin] had ceased to be connected with their life" [that is, with the life of Nicholas and Alexandra]. We have but to read the letters of the Empress to her husband to discover the truth: Rasputin remained the great friend and confidant.

"Our Friend intends to leave for his home about the fifth" (November), wrote Alexandra to Nicholas, in her letter of October 24, "and wants to come to-day." She adds on the next day: "Our Friend came in the evening for an hour; he has decided to wait for your return and will go home for some time only afterwards." On December 16 she says: "I spoke for a minute on the telephone with Grigory. He sends the message: 'Fortitude of the spirit—in a few days I shall be with you and we shall talk about everything.'" To put an end to disgusting rumours, Alexandra preferred to see Rasputin in the privacy of Anna Virubova's house. The Empress's letters are full of references to these meetings: "I saw Anna for a moment. Our Friend came there because He desired to see me" (January 29, 1915), or: "I hope to see our Friend at Anna's for a moment—this will cheer me up" (June 12). We find the above sentence, one of the several hundreds referring to Rasputin scattered in the letters of the Empress, in a letter which begins with the words: "My only one" and ends: "I cover you with tender kisses. Ever yours, your old wifey." Alexandra tells Nicholas: "I long to hold you tightly clasped in my arms with your sweet head resting upon my shoulder. Then I could cover Lovey's face and eyes with kisses and murmur soft words of love. I kiss your cushion at nights—that's all I have—and bless it. Now I must go to sleep. Rest well, my treasure, I bless and kiss you ever so fondly and gently stroke your dear brow." A few lines further we find the sentence: "Forgive me, but I do not like your choice of Minister of War . . . how I wish I were with you and could hear all your reasons for choosing him . . . is he not our Friend's enemy, as that brings bad luck. . . . Lovey mine, tell them [the Ministers] upon their return from Headquarters to ask and see me, one after the other and I shall pray hard and try my utmost to be of real use to you." This is one of the earliest indications of the active part which Alexandra had begun to take in politics and of her ever present anxiety that no appointment should be made contrary to the wishes of Rasputin.

The time was drawing nigh when the interest which Alexandra took in the affairs of Nicholas was destined to become intense, for in the autumn of 1915 the Emperor at last carried out his wish of becoming Commander-in-Chief himself. We have mentioned the popularity of the Grand Duke Nicholas and the growth of his intervention in the affairs of Government. The Emperor had the feeling that if this state of affairs was allowed to continue the Grand Duke would become the Dictator of Russia. In addition, throughout the summer the armies had been steadily retreating before the powerful onslaught of the Germans. Great losses had been incurred, enormous territories had been sacrificed, hundreds of thousands of prisoners had been left in the hands of the enemy and nobody could foretell when the disastrous retreat, rendered all the more tragic by a shortage of arms and munitions, would come to a stop. In justice to Nicholas—and some day this will be placed to his credit by dispassionate historians—it must be said that he desired to place himself at the head of his troops not to enjoy the fruits of a carefully prepared victory, but to share their fate at a critical moment. The ministers of the crown and other trusted statesmen had been unanimous in advising against the change. But the Empress, guided by Rasputin, favoured the change and worked hard to obtain it. The "Man of God" had become the sworn enemy of the Grand Duke from the moment when the latter changed his attitude to-

wards him and tried to obtain his dismissal from
Court. For many months Rasputin had been warning
Alexandra against the ambitious Grand Duke and she
passed on his poisonous remarks to her husband. So,
as far back as September 20, 1914, that is, when the
War was yet developing in a not unsatisfactory
fashion, we read in a letter:

"Our Friend is happy for your sake that you are
gone [to the front] and was so glad to have seen you
yesterday. He always fears Bonheur,[2] that is to say,
the crows,[3] want him to get the Polish throne or
Galicia, that is their aim, but I said she [Anna V.]
should quiet him; even out of thankfulness you would
never risk such a thing. Grigory loves you jealously
and can't bear Nicholas playing a part."

At last in August, 1915, the momentous change
was made and the Czar was installed as Commander-
in-Chief. In a letter dated August 25 he gives an
account of the interview with Grand Duke Nicholas,
when the transfer of powers was accomplished and
adds:

"My dear wifey, think if it is not possible for you
to come to the assistance of your little husband whilst
he is away? What a pity that you did not carry out
this duty long ago, or at least during the war. I do
not know a more agreeable feeling than to be proud
of you, as I was proud of you during these months,

---

[2] Nickname for the Grand Duke Nicholas.
[3] The "black" Grand Duchesses Militza and Stana.

when unceasingly you pressed me to be strong and to stand by my view."

These words are evidently the answer to a letter of Alexandra dated August 22 and which had just reached him. Alexandra was writing immediately after the departure of Nicholas for the front, where he was to replace the Grand Duke. A few days before, several ministers, who had opposed the scheme with all their might had been summarily dismissed from their posts. The heart of Alexandra was overflowing with exultant pride:

Tsarskoe Selo, Aug. 22, 1915

MY VERY OWN BELOVED ONE,

I cannot find words to express all I want to. My heart is far too full. I only long to hold you tight in my arms and whisper words in intense love, courage, strength and endless blessing. More than hard to let you go alone, so completely alone. But God is very near to you, more than ever. You have fought this great fight for your country and throne, alone with bravery and decision. Never have they seen such firmness in you before and it cannot remain without fruit. Do not fear for what remains behind. One must be severe and stop all at once. Lovey, I am here. Don't laugh at silly old wifey, but she has "trousers" on unseen and I can get the old man [the Prime Minister] to come and keep him up to be energetic. Whenever I can be of the smallest use, tell me what to do. Use me, at such a time God will give me strength to help you, because our souls are fighting for the right against evil. It is all much deeper than appears to the eye. We, who have been taught to look at all from another side, see what the struggle here really is and means; you showing your mastery, proving yourself the Autocrat without whom Russia cannot exist. Had you given in now on these different questions, they would have dragged yet more out of you. Being firm is the only salvation. I know what it costs you and have and do suffer hideously for you. Forgive me, I beseech you, my Angel, for having left you no peace and worried you so much, but I know too well your marvellously gentle character and you had to shake it off this time, had to win your fight alone against all. It will be a glorious page in your reign and Russian history, the story of these weeks and days, and God, who is just and near you, will save your country and your throne through your firmness. A harder battle has rarely been fought, than yours and it will be crowned with success, only believe this. Your faith has been tried—your trust—and you remained firm as a rock, for that you will be blessed. God anointed you at your Coronation, He placed you where you stand and you have done your duty, be sure, quite sure of this and He forsaketh not His anointed. Our Friend's prayers arise night and day for you to Heaven and God will hear them. Those, who fear and cannot understand your actions, will be brought by events to realize your great wisdom. It is the beginning of the glory of your reign. He [Rasputin] said so and I absolutely believe it. Your Sun is rising and to-day it shines so brightly. And so will you charm all those great blunderers, cowards, led astray, noisy, blind, narrowminded and false beings this morning. And your Sunbeam [Alexis] will appear to help you, your very own child. Won't that touch those hearts and make them realize what you are doing and what they dared to wish to do, to shake your throne, to frighten you with internal black forebodings; only a bit of success out there and they will change. They will go home into clean air and their minds will be purified and they will carry the picture of you and your son in their hearts with them. . . . All is for the good as our Friend says, the worst is over . . . when you leave, shall wire to Friend through Anya and He will particularly think of you. . . . Tell me the impression if you can. Be firm to the end, let me be sure of that, otherwise shall get quite ill from anxiety. Bitter pain not to be with you. Know what you feel and the meeting with N. [Grand Duke Nicholas] won't be agreeable. You did trust him and now you know what months ago our Friend said that he was acting wrongly towards you and your country and wife. . . . Lovey, if you hear that I am not so well, don't be anxious. I have suffered so terribly and physically overtired myself these two days and morally worried (and worry still till all is done at Headquarters and Nikolasha gone) only then I shall feel calm . . . you see they are afraid of me and so come to you when alone. They know I have a will of my own, when I feel I am in the right, and you are now—we know it— so you make them tremble before your courage and will. God is with you and our Friend for you —all is well—and later all will thank you for having saved the country. Don't doubt—believe,

and all will be well. . . . The Lefts are furious
because all slips through their hands and their
cards are clear to us and the game they wished to
use Nikolasha for. . . . Now goodnight, lovey,
go straight to bed without tea with the rest and
their long faces. Sleep long and well, you need
a rest after this strain and your heart needs calm
hours. God Almighty bless your undertaking,
His holy Angels guard and guide you and bless
the work of your hands. . . . I always place a
candle before St. Nicholas at Znamenje [a
church] for you and shall do so to-morrow at 3
o,cl. and before the Virgin. You will feel my soul
near you. I clasp you tenderly to my heart, kiss
and caress you without end, want to show you all
the intense love I have for you, warm, cheer, con-
sole, strengthen you and make you sure of yourself. Sleep well, my Sunshine, Russia's Saviour.
Remember last night, how tenderly we clung together. I shall yearn for your caresses. I never
can have enough of them. And I still have the
children and you are all alone. Another time I
must give you Baby [Alexis] for a bit to cheer you
up. I kiss you without end and bless you. Holy
Angels guard your slumber. I am near and with
you for ever and none shall separate us.

Your very own wife,
Sunny

The granddaughter of Queen Victoria, after more
than twenty years in Russia, had shed her western
ideas and stood revealed in her oriental mysticism.
Her faith in God was a real thing indeed, but it was

curiously blended with veneration for "our Friend" and with a lot of native superstition. The pact of autocracy with heaven stood as firm as ever now that Nicholas had found his nerve again and was ready to act as a master before whom his subjects must tremble. The transformation of the shy Alix into the imperious Alexandra was complete: she was conscious of possessing the unlimited courage and determination which her husband lacked, and she was now ready to employ them. It is not for nothing that she spoke about her "invisible breeches." Nicholas had been given by heaven a mission to fulfil and Alexandra would see that he remained firm in his resolution to do his duty. While he was away at Headquarters directing military operations the Empress would look after the ministers and see that they did not pander to the odious Left or do anything contrary to the wishes of "Our Friend."

Rasputin was at the height of his influence. Not a day passed without the Empress consulting him on one question or another. While Nicholas was away the "Man of God" came to the Palace very rarely, but he was a constant guest at the house of Anna Virubova or communicated with the Empress by telephone. The letters of Alexandra show that Rasputin took an interest in the most various things: the appointment of bishops, the food supply, railway loans, the liberation of a speculator arrested by the military authorities and the conduct of the war. The latter apparently was of great interest to him. Not only was he

anxious to know all about the situation but he gave
important advice: where to attack and when.

"Now, before I forget, I must give you a message
from our Friend, prompted by what He saw in the
night. He begs you to order that one should advance near Riga; says it is necessary; otherwise the
Germans will settle down so firmly through the winter that it will cost endless bloodshed and trouble to
make them move. Now it will take them so aback
that we shall succeed in making them retrace their
steps—He says this is just now the most essential
thing and begs you seriously to order ours to advance,
he says we can and we must and I was to write it to
you at once."

From day to day the power of the Empress grew.
Inspired by Rasputin she resisted all attempts to give
the country ministers having the confidence of the
Duma—the elected legislative assembly. Instead,
unworthy men or incapable ones were appointed and
the qualification asked from them was a conviction
in the sanctity of the autocratic principle and a friendly
relationship with Rasputin. The discontent in the
country grew apace and the most horrible rumours
were flying about the Empress. The latter was in a
state of perpetual anger:

"A private husband would not one hour stand these
assaults upon his wife. Personally, I do not care
a straw. When I was young I suffered horribly
through those injustices said about me, oh how often.
But now the worldly things don't touch me deeply,

I mean nastinesses. They [the public] will come round some day, only my Huzzy ought really to stick up for me a bit, as many think you don't care and hide behind me." [4]

It was tragic. Since the spring of 1915 the Russians, fighting bravely all the time, had been pressed back and back by the overwhelming superiority of the Germans in artillery. The official reports about a "withdrawal to prepared positions" appeared with a monotonous regularity. But they were supplemented by private information and rumours about an appalling deficiency in shells and even rifle ammunition. Thousands of prisoners were left each day in the hands of the enemy and often there were no rifles available for the reinforcements, which were rushed to the fighting line. The nation was horror-stricken by the discovery of the fact that the Ministry for War and its subordinate departments had neglected to take steps to develop the production of munitions or to supply the heavy guns of which the army stood in great need. It became known that Grand Duke Nicholas and his Staff for months had been warning the bureaucrats

---

[4] The letters of Alexandra are full of references to Rasputin's views and wishes. In addition to those already given the following are chosen as illuminating: "To follow our Friend's counsels, love, is right. I assure you. He prays so hard day and night for you and He has kept you where you are. Only be as convinced as I am. Then all will go well. In *Les Amis des Dieux* [a book recommended to Alexandra by Philippe] one of the old men of God said that a country, where a 'Man of God' helps the Sovereign, will never be lost. . . ." (Letter No. 632, December 5, 1916.) And again: "Be the master; listen to your staunch wifey and our Friend . . ." (December 6, 1916). In all there are four hundred and twenty-two references to Rasputin in the letters of Alexandra, which are in our possession.

at home about the coming scarcity of supplies, but
had been unable to break through their red tape and
lazy habits. Now at last alive to the danger, the best
men of the nation demanded the right to intervene.
The officials were obliged to confess their impotence
and for once the Government was forced to appeal to
the nation for assistance. The appeal met with an im-
mediate enthusiastic response and, led by the political
circles grouped around the Duma, a mighty and successful effort was developed to supply the material
needs of the army. The enthusiasm which had en-
flamed the nation in the summer of 1914 broke out
afresh and the commanders in the field and their
troops, heartened by the support they were receiving,
faced the enemy with renewed energy and resolved
now to take their revenge. But the enhanced position
of the Duma and the growing influence of democratic
circles in the affairs of Government were not to the
taste of the Empress, who saw in them a great danger
for the autocratic principle of which she had constituted herself the guardian.

During the fateful year 1916 Nicholas was absent
from home for more than six months and the letters
and telegrams of Alexandra, written during that
period, supply us with a mass of information, confirming the view that the Empress had acquired a real
influence over the affairs of Government and especially
over the appointment of ministers. Nicholas himself
is witness to this fact in the following remarkable
letter:

The Tragic Bride

Imperial Headquarters, September 23, 1916

MY LOVE,

I thank you tenderly for your dear long letter in which you describe so well your conversation with Protopopoff.[5] With the help of God he will be the man we need at present. . . . Yes, really, you must be my eyes and ears there, in the capital, whilst I am obliged to sit here. It is your duty to maintain the accord and unity among the Ministers—thus you are of enormous assistance to me and our country. Oh incomparable Sunny, I am so happy that at last you have found a suitable occupation. Naturally, now I shall be at rest and need not worry at least about internal affairs. . . . For ever your old

NICKY

Nevertheless it is precisely the "internal affairs" about which Nicholas had ceased to worry which were going from bad to worse. The ministers appointed by Alexandra lacked experience, tact and did not possess any of the qualities of statesmanship. They were not even capable of carrying out effectively the reactionary measures which on the demand of the Empress they promulgated against the democratic elements in the country. While at the front the situation was shaping for the better, the position inside Russia was becoming increasingly dangerous. Wide circles were drawn into active opposition to the plan of the Empress to crush the legislative assembly and to prepare for the return of a really autocratic

---

[5] Minister of the Interior, a creature and adherent of Rasputin.

régime. Staunch adherents of the monarchy and even members of the Imperial family became alarmed at the course of events. They warned, they entreated, but Nicholas was engrossed by military affairs and saw the internal situation through the eyes of Alexandra, who kept blindly to the chosen reactionary policy. The Monarchists saw the danger of an imminent revolution, which would sweep away not only Nicholas but the throne itself. They—there is now no doubt about this—discussed a plan for effecting themselves a revolution at the Palace by seizing the person of the Empress and obliging Nicholas either to consent to a separation from her or to abdicate himself in favour of his brother Michael. But, while there was much loose talk on the subject, a few hotheads decided to solve the problem by destroying Rasputin, in whom they saw the inspirer of the fatal policy pursued by the Empress. The Grand Duke Dimitry, a cousin, and Prince Yusupoff, who had married a niece of the Emperor, were among the conspirators. Rasputin was enticed late at night to Yusupoff's house and there killed under atrocious circumstances in the midst of an orgy. The story of the murder has been told by its perpetrators. Rasputin put up a hard, an unbelievable, resistance to death. The deadly poison, which had been put in his wine, did not produce any apparent effect on his sturdy organism and the panic-stricken conspirators then put bullets into him, which seemed unable to end his life. Stricken down and left for dead, Rasputin staggered up again and made for the door to get away. Finally he was finished off by a shot in the back. His body was taken away and thrown into a hole in the ice in the Neva estuary. But the expected moral effect of the assassination was not attained. We ascribe this first of all to the fact that the revolutionary situation had developed too far to be influenced by the disappearance of Rasputin and also to the moral cowardice of the conspirators, who, instead of declaring openly what they had done and facing the consequences in a court of law, began by denying the act and then availed themselves of their privileged position to escape the ordinary course of the law by going into banishment.

On December 14, 1916, Alexandra had just finished a letter to her husband, a despondent letter, for she had a feeling of intense lassitude and complained of her heart. She wanted her husband to come to her:

> At such a time to be separated I assure you is at times absolutely exasperating and distracting. How much easier to have shared all together and spoken over everything, instead of letters, which have less force, alas, and often must have aggravated you, my poor patient Angel. But I have to try and be the antidote to the poison of others.

Then come lines—disjointed words—thrown on to the paper anyhow in pencil:

> We are sitting all together—can imagine our feelings—thoughts—Our Friend has disappeared. Yesterday A [Anna] saw Him and He said

The Empress Rules

Felix [Yusupoff] asked Him to come in the night, a motor would fetch Him to see Irina [Yusupoff had promised to make Rasputin acquainted with his wife]—a motor fetched Him [military motor] with two civilians and he drove away. This night big scandal at Yusupoff's house—big meeting, Dimitry [Grand Duke], Purishkevitch [a member of the Duma], etc.—all drunk. Police heard shots. Purishkevitch ran out screaming to the police that our Friend was killed. Police searching and Justice entered now into Yusupoff's house—did not dare before as Dimitry there—Chief of police has sent for Dimitry. Felix wished to leave to-night for Crimea—I begged Kalinin [nickname for Protopopoff] to stop him—Our Friend was in good spirits but nervous these days. . . . Felix pretends He never came to the house and never asked him. Seems quite a paw. I still trust in God's mercy that one has only driven Him off somewhere. Kalinin is doing all he can. . . . Shall keep her [Anna] to live here—as now they will get at her next. Such utter anguish. Am calm and can't believe it. God have mercy. I cannot and won't believe He has been killed. Thanks for dear letter, come quickly—nobody will dare touch her or do anything when you are here. Felix came often to Him lately.

I bless and kiss you,
SUNNY

For two days Alexandra lived in the hope that "God's mercy" would protect her "friend." She sent desperate telegrams to Nicholas imploring him to come to her: "I ardently desire your presence, God help us." "I hope you will leave to-day as I need you terribly," and then: "When are you coming?" The Emperor hurriedly transferred his duties to his Chief-of-Staff and left for Tsarskoe Selo. At one of the stations on the way he was given a telegram from his wife: "Found in the water. Thoughts, prayers together, Alix," for the body of Rasputin had been discovered under the ice. It was taken away by police, placed in a sumptuous coffin and secretly conveyed to Tsarskoe Selo, where the Empress had decided that it should be buried in a new church she was having built.

To illustrate the loss to Alexandra and to Nicholas occasioned by the death of Rasputin we shall quote only a few words from a letter, which shows the place held by the "Man of God" in their life. Writing on November 5, 1916, Alexandra says:

"Our Friend is so angry Olga married.[6] He finds she did wrong towards you and that can bring her no luck."

This interference by Rasputin in the intimate affairs of the family, an interference which to Alexandra appeared quite natural, is more illuminating than any long political tirade. Rasputin's influence penetrated the whole life of Alexandra and his loss was a blow which upset what remained to her at the time of her mental balance.

---

[6] Grand Duchess Olga, youngest sister of the Emperor, divorced her first husband the Duke of Oldenburg and married a simple officer, Kulikowsky.

CHAPTER XVII

THE REVOLUTION

HE autocratic régime in Russia had worn itself out and as it would not and could not introduce the necessary measure of democratic reform the Revolution became inevitable. But we may well ask: why did it come in the spring of 1917 and why did it take the form it did?

Four days before Rasputin's terrible death Alexandra wrote to her husband:

My Angel,

We dined yesterday at A [Anna]'s with our Friend. It was so nice, we told all about our journey [the Empress had just come back from a visit to the hospitals and churches in the ancient city of Novgorod] and He said we ought to have gone straight to you as we would have brought you intense joy and blessing. And I feared disturbing you. He entreats you to be firm, to be the Master and not always to give in to Trepov.[1] You know

---

[1] Prime Minister, appointed by Nicholas from Headquarters for once without consulting Alexandra. Rasputin viewed Trepov with disfavour and he was soon replaced by Prince Gilitizine, a senile courtier, who was destined to be the last Prime Minister of a senile régime.

all much better than that man. Still you let him lead you. Why not our Friend who leads through God? Remember why I am disliked; shows it right to be firm and feared, and you be the same, you a man. Only believe more in our Friend. He lives for you and Russia. And we must give a strong country to Baby and dare not be weak for his sake, else he will have a yet harder reign, setting our faults to right and drawing the reins in tightly, which you let loose. You have to suffer for faults in the reigns of your predecessors and, God knows what hardships are yours. Let our legacy be lighter for Alexei. He has a strong mind and will of his own, don't let things slip through your fingers and make him to build up again. Be firm: I, your wall, am behind you and won't give way, I know He leads us right, and you listen to a false man like Trepov. Only out of love which you bear for me and Baby, take no steps without warning me and speaking over all quietly. Would I write thus, did I not know you so very easily waver and change your mind and what it costs to make you stick to your opinion. I know I may hurt you how I write—that is my pain and sorrow—but you, Baby and Russia are far too dear to me. . . . Only not a responsible Ministry which all are mad about. It's all getting calmer and better, only one wants to feel your hand. For many years people have told me: "Russia loves the knout." It's their nature: tender love and then the iron hand to punish and guide. How I wish I could pour my will into your veins. The Holy Virgin is above you, for you, with you. Remember the miracle—our Friend's vision. . . . Forgive this letter, but I could not sleep this night worrying over you. Don't hide things from me; I am strong. But listen to me, which means our Friend and trust us through all and beware of Trepov. . . . I suffer over you as over a tender, softhearted child, which needs guiding, but listens to bad advisers, whilst a Man of God tells him what to do. Sweetest Angel, come home soon. . . . Love boundless, therefore seems harsh all I write; pardon, believe and understand, I love you two [Nicholas and Alexis] too deeply and cry over your faults and rejoice over every right step. God bless and protect, guard and guide you. Kisses without end.

Your truest

WIFEY

Nicholas' answer to this appeal was as follows:

MY DARLING,

Tender thanks for the severe reprimand in writing. I read it with a smile because you talk to me as to a child. It is disgusting to have to do with a man whom I do not like and whom I do not trust like Trepov. But first a successor must be found and then he can be got rid of, but when he has done the dirty work. I mean to dismiss him after he has closed the Duma. Let the whole responsibility and all the difficulties rest on his shoulders and not on the shoulders of the man who will take his place. . . . God bless you my soul, my Sunny. I kiss you tenderly, as well as the girls, and remain your "poor, little, weak husband."

NICKY

The Tragic Bride

These two letters furnish the explanation, why the Revolution had to be. They disclose such a misunderstanding of the whole political situation, which we would qualify as criminal if it were not so evidently sincere. But it is clear that with such rulers—childish, petty, superstitious and blind to all that was going on—autocracy was doomed, because there was no autocracy left worth speaking about. The physical disappearance of Rasputin could not alter the situation, for his spirit continued to reign over the mind of Alexandra. When Nicholas, who had rushed home at the news of Rasputin's death, was leaving for the front again after two months wasted in an effort to consolidate the régime [2] he found on the writing desk in his compartment in the train a letter which Alexandra had laid there for him to read:

---

[2] Rodzianko, the President of the Duma, says in his memoirs that he saw the Emperor a few days before his departure from Tsarskoe Selo. Rodzianko had the courage to warn Nicholas of the dangerous position: "Your Majesty . . . I consider the state of the country to have become more critical and menacing than ever. The spirit of the people is such that the gravest upheavals may be expected. Parties exist no longer and all Russia is unanimous in claiming a change of Government and the appointment of a responsible Premier invested with the confidence of the nation. . . . As if purposely, everything is done to the detriment of Russia and the advantage of her enemies. No wonder monstrous rumours are afloat of treason and espionage in the rear of the army. Sire, there is not a single honest or reliable man left in your entourage; all the best have either been eliminated or have resigned; and only those who have bad reputations have remained. It is an open secret that the Empress issues orders without your knowledge, that Ministers report to her on matters of State, and that by her wish those whom she views with disfavour lose their posts and are replaced by incompetent and inexperienced persons. Indignation against and hatred of the Empress are growing throughout the country. . . ."

The Revolution

MY PRECIOUS DARLING,

With sadness and deep anxiety I have allowed you to leave alone without our dear tender Baby. What a terrible time we are passing through. To be separated increases the suffering: I cannot fondle you, when you look so tired, so worn out. Verily God has sent you a terribly heavy cross. My passionate desire is to help you to carry this burden. You are brave and patient—with all my heart and soul I suffer with you, much more than I can express in words. What can I do? Only pray and pray. Our dear Friend in another world is also praying for you. Thus he is nearer to us than before. But oh how I would like to hear his consoling and encouraging voice. God will help, I am sure, and will give you a great reward for all you have suffered. But how long has one to wait. It looks as if things were getting better. Only, my darling, be firm, show the hand of the Master. This is what the Russians need. Never have you missed the occasion of being kind, to show love and kindness—let them feel now sometimes your fist. How many have told me: "We need the knout"—they ask for it themselves. Curiously enough such is the Slav nature. . . . They must learn to fear you—to love is not sufficient. . . .

This frenzied appeal for firmness and action was more necessary than the Empress imagined. If anything could save the throne it was courageous action: either the granting of a responsible parliamentary Government, which would have rallied, even at this

241

eleventh hour, the major part of the nation, or the employment of repressive measures for which, if decided upon, there could have been yet found the executive power. But the autocracy did neither and, while it stood at the crossways, fate overtook it and swept it away with an ease, which surprised the world. Unfortunately, democracy, which should have taken the situation in hand, was swept away together with the monarchy. This came about in the following manner.

We have said already that the War was, in the beginning, the occasion for a revival of the union between the Emperor and the nation. Patriotic fervour, reborn, provided a powerful backing to the action of the armies in the field. Single defeats, however painful, were not able to shake the national resolution to see the struggle through to the end, the ultimate victory being never in doubt. Then came the great retreat of 1915, when for more than six months the Russians, shamefully left in the lurch by the bureaucratic servants of autocracy, had been obliged by a dearth of munitions to give way before the victorious Germans. Again the nation, when called to the rescue, jumped into the breach and by a valiant effort not only stemmed the tide of defeat, but prepared for a final victory. But the recompense vouchsafed to the democratic effort was a renewal of an autocratic policy inspired by the blinded Empress and carried out by the stupid ministers appointed under her influence. Proud of its patriotic achievement democracy expected to receive at last a share in the government in the form of a cabinet responsible to the legislative assembly. This modest and fair demand was treated with contempt from the throne. Monarchy and democracy, instead of availing themselves of the heaven-sent opportunity to compose their differences and unite their forces, treated each other as enemies, preparing to destroy one another. They did not see that a third force—anarchy—had grown up ready to annihilate them both.

The idea of the military authorities had always been to have in hand as large a number as possible of reserves to fill in the gaps continuously occurring in the fighting front. In pursuance of this policy the number of men called up had been from the beginning much greater than immediately necessary and, literally, millions of reservists and recruits were accumulated in the camps and barracks all over the country. As there were not arms enough to keep the front supplied, the rear was denuded of them completely and the reserves in consequence could not be trained. In addition there was a lack of good officers. The commanding cadres of the old army, which went into the War in 1914, had been splendid, but they had been used up lavishly during the first hectic months without any thought for the future. In opposition to the economic methods of the Germans, Russian regiments prided themselves upon marching into battle with all their officers in the front rank. In consequence very soon few of these were left and a mass of youngsters was promoted after a short course of superficial training. The officers belonged mostly to the class of the Russian intelligentzia, whose moral characteristics did not make them eminently suitable for the part of leaders of men. But even of these there was not a sufficient number and, the fighting front taking all the available material, there was none left for the reserves in the country. The author himself once had the experience of a camp, in which for forty thousand men and more, crowded together, there were only *eighteen* officers and of the latter only *two* had been to the war. The situation in regard to non-commissioned officers was even worse. Thus it came about that behind the front there were millions of strong healthy men, eating their hearts out in inactivity, untrained, undisciplined and in addition well fed. This latter consideration is of importance. The sale of alcoholic drinks had been stopped all over the country on the day of the declaration of war; the Russian peasant of whom the army naturally consisted to more than ninety per cent was given a diet much richer than he had been accustomed to. He received a daily meat allowance, when perhaps in ordinary times he was able to afford it on very rare occasions during the year. Abundantly fed and left to his own devices the soldier in the reserve camps and barracks tended to become a hulking brute, open to all suggestions insidiously put before him by unscrupulous agitators. Of the latter there was an abundance.

Subversive propaganda among the troops of the

enemy was practised by all the belligerents, but by none with such conspicuous success as by the Germans in Russia. For they had at their disposal a large native contingent composed principally of the worst elements in the old revolutionary parties, the best men in which had ceased their activities for the time of the War. The autocratic régime had nothing to oppose to this propaganda. In its incredible blindness it pinned its faith to the "traditional attachment of the simple peasant to the Czar" and literally did nothing to make this "attachment" a living thing based on patriotic conviction. On this subject the author can speak from personal experience. In December, 1916, that is, less than two months before the fatal revolutionary outbreak, he came to St. Petersburg, or Petrograd as it had become then, after several years' absence at the front. To his intense surprise he quickly discovered that the garrison of the capital consisted of about one hundred thousand reservists, badly trained, thinly officered, herded in barracks and worked upon openly by a subversive propaganda. Even worse: In Tsarskoe Selo near by, there were perhaps fifty thousand more troops of the same category and not a single well officered fighting regiment. And this was the residence of the Emperor and of his family! An enemy of the régime could not have done worse for it than it did for itself. The experienced officials of the political police, coldly calculating the chances, had reported, early in January, 1917, that the situation was "amazingly similar to that which prevailed in

1905 before the revolutionary outbreak." But the Government seemed unable to see reason. Protopopoff, the inept Minister of the Interior, a creature of Rasputin and therefore protected by the Empress, conceived the insane idea, instead of preventing popular riots from happening, to take advantage of them for inflicting a salutary lesson on the "Republicans." This criminal scheme was the direct cause of the disaster to the throne in February.

On February 24 the Empress wrote:

": . . There were disorders yesterday on the Vassily Ostroff and on the Nevsky [3] because the poor people stormed the bakeries. They have broken Philippof's [a famous bakery on the Nevsky Prospect] into smithereens and the Cossacks were called out against them. All this has come to my knowledge unofficially. . . ."

The Empress does not seem to have attached a great importance to these disorders. Her letter is principally concerned with a description of the measles from which Alexis, the two elder daughters and Anna Virubova were suffering. An interesting sentence is the following: "Do not forget to write to Georgie [H. M. King George V] about Buchanan." [4] Pro-

---

[3] Vassily Ostroff is an island in the Neva estuary on which is one of the oldest parts of St. Petersburg; the Nevsky Prospect is the principal street in the city, built round with imposing mansions and palaces.

[4] Sir George Buchanan, British Ambassador to the Russian Court, with whom Alexandra was extremely displeased because of his alleged close connection with politicians of the Left. Sir George Buchanan had the courage to warn the Emperor of the dangerous

topopoff had known about the probable outbreak of these disorders beforehand and is credited with the idea of allowing them to develop and to take a sufficiently serious turn—this would have authorized shooting by the troops, which were concentrated in readiness for action. The Cossacks who had been called out to deal with the mob showed signs of a fractious spirit and in several places refused to co-operate with the police in obliging the people to disperse. The author has preserved in his memory a small but characteristic detail: on the morning of that day he was at his dentist's and his visit was cut short because the hall porter came up to say that a policeman had been round to order the front door to be locked "as there would be shooting." During the day the main streets and bridges were guarded by detachments of troops, which did not appear excited and armoured cars drove about in an aimless manner. The police were very active but the military authorities appeared listless and anxious to avoid a clash. On the next day the Empress wrote again:

". . . the strikes and disorders in town are more than bold. . . . It is a houligan movement, boys and girls run about and shout that they have no bread—simply to cause· excitement—and workmen, who prevent others from working. If the weather were cold, they all, probably, would remain at home. All will

---

situation in the country and especially of the fact that the Empress was fiercely and universally hated, and that all circles were clamouring for her removal.

pass and quieten down if the Duma will do the right thing. . . ."

The major part of the letter deals again with the illness of the children, with the fact that the Empress has been obliged to receive uninteresting people: "a Chinaman, a Portuguese with two daughters, a Greek and an Argentinian with his wife." These members of the diplomatic corps were the last to have an audience with the Empress, for the situation had become suddenly much worse. In the letter of February 26 we find:

> . . . Told me much about the riots in town—I think more than 200,000 men . . . it is necessary to introduce the card system for bread as has been done already in all countries. This has been done for sugar and all are quiet and receive enough. People here are idiots. . . . A poor gendarme officer was killed by the mob and also several others. All the trouble comes from the gaping public, well dressed people, wounded soldiers, etc., girl students, etc., who instigate others. . . . I have just been with Marie to Snamenja [5] to place candles [before the icons], walked to the tomb of our Friend. The walls of the church are now so high that I can kneel and pray for you all without the sentinel seeing me. . . . I brought away for you this little piece of wood from His tomb, where I knelt. In town yesterday the position was not good. One hundred and twenty to one hundred and thirty people have been arrested . . . the

[5] A church being built by the Empress.

Ministers and several members of the Right of the Duma have been in consultation last night about the severe measures to be taken and all hope that to-morrow all will be calm. . . . It looks to me that all will be well. The sun is shining so brightly and I felt so calm and peaceful at His dear tomb. He died to save us. . . .

The Emperor had telegraphed that he was returning to St. Petersburg and the Empress apparently ceased writing, therefore, for we do not possess any letters of hers for the next few days. Events in the capital began to develop with a lightninglike rapidity. The mob was becoming more aggressive every minute and signs multiplied of deep disaffection among the troops. The ministers were paralyzed with fright and incapable of concerted or sane action. The only hope was that the Duma would take the situation in hand. For this it was necessary that the Emperor should agree to the formation of a cabinet responsible to the legislative assembly. Instead Prince Galitzine, the Prime Minister, communicated to the President of the Duma, Rodzianko, an Imperial *ukase* ordering a suspension of the session. But already one regiment had revolted and was marching to the Duma. Not a moment was to be lost and the Duma, disregarding the decree for its prorogation, formed an executive committee charged with the restoration of order. The revolt of the garrison became general, the arsenal was stormed by soldiers and workmen who seized a great quantity of arms. Looting started in places, outrages were committed against officers and officials and socialist groups set up a council of soldiers and workers' deputies, with the avowed intention of proclaiming a Republic. To save the situation Rodzianko, a fervent monarchist himself, consented to the setting up by the Duma of a provisional government. Commissioners took charge of the various departments, which were surrendered to them without a struggle by the ministers.

On March 2 Alexandra, without news from her husband and worried to distraction by the march of events, dispatched two young officers to find the Emperor and gave to each a letter written on a small square of paper in a tiny envelope. It is characteristic of her that in spite of her anxiety she did not forget to number these letters, as was her custom. Their text has been preserved for history.

March 2, 1917

MY BELOVED, MY PRECIOUS ANGEL, LIGHT OF MY
    LIFE,

My heart breaks at the thought that you are completely alone, suffering this torture and anxiety, and that we know nothing about you, and you know nothing about us. I am now sending to you Solovieff and Gramotin. I give a letter to each and hope that one, at least, will reach you. I wanted to send an aeroplane, but all the men have disappeared. The young men will tell you all, so that I need not write about the situation. All is horrid and events are developing

with a colossal swiftness. But I am convinced
—and nothing can move this faith—that all will
be well. Particularly since I have received your
telegram this morning[6] the first ray of sun in
this morass. Not knowing where you were, I
took action through Headquarters, because
Rodzianko tried to make me believe that he did
not know why you were held up. Clearly, they
do not want to let you see me unless you
sign some paper, a constitution or some other
horror like that. And you, all alone, without
the backing of the army, caught like a mouse
in a trap, what can you do? This is the greatest
infamy and a low down trick, unheard of in history: to arrest the sovereign. P. [?] cannot now
reach you because Luga[7] is taken by the revolutionaries. They have held up, overpowered
and disarmed the [?] regiment and spoilt the line.
Perhaps you will show yourself to the troops in
Pskov and in other places and will collect them
around you. If you are forced to make concessions you are in no case obliged to carry them
out, because they have been obtained from you
in a shameful fashion. . . . We all are in good
spirits and not broken by circumstances, only we
are anxious for you and feel unspeakably hurt
for your sake, my holy martyr. God Almighty
may He assist you.

Last night between one and half past two I saw
Ivanoff, who is now here in his train.[8] I thought

---

[6] This was the first news from the Emperor for three days. His
train trying to get past the blockade of the Revolutionaries had been
trying various lines of approach and at last had been held up at
Pskov, about two hundred miles from St. Petersburg.

[7] A railway station, halfway between St. Petersburg and Pskov.

[8] General Ivanoff had been dispatched by Nicholas from Head-

he could get to you through Dno [a railway junction], but can he break through? He hoped to bring your train in behind his own. The house of Fredericks [Minister of the Court] has been burnt, his family is in the Horse-Guards hospital. . . . There are two currents: the Duma and the revolutionaries—two snakes, which, so I hope, will tear off each other's heads—this would save the situation. I have a feeling that God will do something. What a brilliant sun to-day. If only you were here. A bad thing is that even our sailors [9] have left us this evening. They do not understand anything, there is some germ in them. . . . When the troops will learn that you are kept a prisoner they will become furious and rise against all. They believe yet that the Duma wants to be with you and for you. Well let them [the Duma] restore order and prove that they can do something. But the fire they have lit is too great, how can they put it out now? . . . I am now going out to speak to the soldiers who are standing in front of the house. I do not know what to write, too many impressions and there is too much to be said. My heart aches very much—I do not pay any attention—my spirit is high and ready to fight. Only I am afraid for you. Now I must end and begin the second letter in case you do not receive this one. It must be small so that they

---

quarters with several battalions of troops reputed loyal to protect the Empress at Tsarskoe. When he arrived there he found the station in the power of the mutineers. He managed in the dead of night to penetrate to the Palace and see the Empress, who forbade him to risk bloodshed in trying to rescue her.

[9] The sailors of the Guard were considered particularly attached to the persons of the Imperial family.

could hide it in a boot, or burn it if necessary.
. . . We all kiss, kiss you without end. God will
help, help and your glory will return. This is the
height of misfortune. How awful for the
Allies and what joy for the enemy. I cannot
give advice, my darling, only be yourself. If
it will be necessary to submit to circumstance, God
will help to obtain freedom. Oh, my holy
martyr. Always with you, ever yours

WIFEY

This letter supplies the proof of the noble courage
which animated the Empress. Hers was a highly
tempered spirit, which prompted her to go where the
danger was greatest. "I am now going out to speak
to the soldiers, who are standing in front of the
house." This short sentence is the only mention made
by Alexandra of a highly dramatic incident. The garrison of Tsarskoe Selo had decided to follow the example of their comrades in St. Petersburg. A mob
of armed men started for the Palace. A sentry who
tried to stop them was struck down. But two com-
panies of the Guard and a few sailors and Cossacks
were yet faithful and took up a position in front of
the Palace to protect it against the mutineers. Gilliard as an eyewitness tells us that the Empress was
horror struck at the thought that blood would be
shed before her door. She took her youngest daughter Marie by the hand and with her went among the
faithful troops, exhorting them to keep cool until the
last moment so as to avoid fighting if possible. Fortunately the firm attitude of the faithful few so impressed

the mob that it withdrew. The Empress went back
to her children, who were lying in darkened rooms
slowly recovering from the severe attack of measles.
Gilliard who watched her with passionate sympathy
remarks: "The Tsarina's despair almost defied
imagination, but her great courage did not desert her.
Her face was terrible to see, but with a strength of
will which was almost superhuman, she had forced
herself to come to the children's rooms as usual so
that the young invalids should suspect nothing. No
one can have any idea of what the Tsarina suffered
during these days, when she was despairing at her
son's bedside and had no news of the Tsar. She
reached the extreme limits of human resistance in this
last trial, in which originated that wonderful and
radiant serenity which was to sustain her and her
family to the day of her death."

On the next day Alexandra found the means of sending another letter:

March 3, 1917

MY BELOVED, SOUL OF MY SOUL, MY WEE ONE,

Oh, how my heart bleeds for you. I am going
mad absolutely without news, apart from disgusting rumours, which can make a person mad. I
should like to know if the two youths whom I sent
to you with letters, have reached you? This letter
will be brought by the wife of an officer. Oh,
for God's sake, just a line. I do not know anything about you, only heart-tearing rumours.
You, without doubt, hear the like. . . . Lovey
mine, lovey. All will be, all must be well,

I do not waver in my faith. My dearest angel,
I love you so, I am always with you, by night and
day. I understand what your poor heart has to
suffer. God have mercy and send you force and
wisdom. He will not leave you. He will help
and reward for these mad sufferings and for the
separation at a time, when it is so necessary to
be together. . . . When shall we be together?
Now we are completely separated and torn away
from each other. . . . Sunny blesses, prays,
keeps to her faith and lives for the sake of her
martyr. She does not interfere in anything. She
has not seen anybody of "those," has never
asked for this. Don't believe if they tell you anything. Now she is only a mother with her sick
children. She cannot do anything because she
fears to cause harm, because she has no news from
her dear one. Such sunny weather too, not a
single cloud. This means : believe and hope. All
is black around, as if at night, but God is above
all. We do not know His ways or how He can
help, but He will hear all the prayers. I do not
know anything about the war. I am cut off
from the world. All the time new, maddening
rumours. The last one : that the father [*i.e.*,
Nicholas] has refused to occupy the post he has
occupied for 23 years. One can lose one's reason, but we shall not lose it. She will believe
in a bright future yet on earth. Remember that

While the Empress was writing these words, the
uncle of the Emperor, the Grand Duke Paul, was
announced. He had come to tell her about Nicholas'
abdication. The Emperor in his train, held up at

Pskov, had met the delegates of the Duma, and after some hesitation had, in his own name and in that of his son, abdicated in favour of his younger brother Michael. Alexandra tearfully added the following words to her letter:

> Paul has just been and has told me all. I perfectly understand your action, my hero. I know that you could not sign anything contrary to your oath at the Coronation.[10] We know each other absolutely, we do not need words, and, I swear by my life, we shall yet see you on the throne, exalted again by your people and your troops for the glory of your reign. You have saved the reign of your son, and the country, and your holy purity and God Himself will crown you on this earth in your country. I embrace you strongly and will never permit them to approach your luminous soul. I kiss, kiss, kiss you, I bless you and always understand you.

After the abdication Nicholas was allowed to send a few words by telegram to his wife and to speak to her on the long-distance telephone. This we see from Alexandra's letter of March 4:

> MY DARLING, MY BELOVED TREASURE,
> This lady is leaving only to-day. She did not leave yesterday. So I can write some more. What a relief, what joy it was to hear your dear voice. Only I could hear very badly and also all conversations are now being tapped.

---

[10] The Empress refers to the pact with heaven to which she attached great importance and which, in her view, made it impossible for Nicholas to grant a constitution.

And your dear telegram this morning. . . .
Baby is bending across the bed and asks me to
give you his kiss. All four are lying in the
green room in darkness. My beloved, my dear
angel, I am afraid to think of what your sufferings are at present. This makes me mad. Oh,
God. Surely, He will recompense you hundred-
fold for your sufferings. I must not write any
more about this. Impossible. How they have
insulted you by sending those two beasts.[11] I
did not know who they were until you told me.
yourself. I feel that the army must rise. . . .

But nobody raised a finger. It is a remarkable fact
that, after his abdication, Nicholas was permitted to
go back in his train to the front unaccompanied by a
representative of the Provisional Government and
absolutely free of his movements. If he had so desired or if it had been practicable Nicholas could have
placed himself at the head of an army corps to march
on St. Petersburg, from where the revolutionary movement had not yet had the time really to spread to
the rest of the country. But everybody at Headquarters seemed to take the abdication as granted. So
worn out had the régime become that its end appeared
natural. But it is also true that the Provisional Government had hostages for Nicholas' good behaviour in
his wife and children at Tsarskoe Selo. After a few
days passed at Headquarters to liquidate the affairs

---

[11] The delegates of the Duma were Gutchkoff and Shulgin, specially
hateful to the Empress because of their fight against the influence of
Rasputin.

of the Supreme Command, Nicholas was brought back under guard to the Palace at Tsarskoe Selo. As the motor car, in which he was driving, reached the gateway, the sentinel shouted: "Open for the Colonel Romanoff."

CHAPTER XVIII

CALVARY

HE Czars of the Lenin dynasty, who from the Kremlin rule over an enslaved land, preserve in their secret archives a copy-book. Bound in black oilcloth it is contained in a cloth case of pale lilac colour with an exotic flower embroidered on the cover. On the first page inside are the words in English:

> *To my sweet Mamma dear*
> *with my best wishes for*
> *a happy New Year.*
> *May God's Blessing be upon you*
> *and guard you for ever.*
> *From your loving girl*
> Tatiana.
> Tobolsk, 1918

At the bottom of the page are added the words in Russian *"Gubernatorsky Dom"*—Governor's House. In this building were imprisoned Nicholas and his family during their detention in Siberia. The copy-book was the Grand Duchess's New Year's present for her mother, who made use of it to write her diary. The last inscription is of July 16 at ten o'clock P.M., that is, only a few hours before the unfortunate

259

prisoners were shot down in the cellar by their assassins. We read:

"Baby has a slight cold. Tatyana is reading the Bible. She has read out to me the book of the prophet Amos. Every morning the commandant comes to our room. He brought me a few eggs for Baby. We had supper at 8 o'clock and I played bézique with Nicholas."

The Grand Duchess reads in her melodious voice:

"In that day will I raise up the tabernacle of David that is fallen and close up the breaches thereof; and I will raise up his ruins and I will build it as in the days of old" (Amos 9:11).

We see the Empress, laying aside the embroidery with which she is eternally busy. Removing her spectacles—her eyes have been strained by hot tears shed in secret—she falls into a reverie. The words of the prophet about the tabernacle which shall be raised again, have for her a special significance. The pact with heaven, which her husband concluded at his coronation cannot be dead. God will perform the miracle and the old glory will return. Alexandra's faith in Providence is as robust as ever. In a letter smuggled out of prison [1] she wrote:

"Yes, separation is a dreadful thing, but God gives strength to bear even this and I feel the Father's [Rasputin's] presence near me and a wonderful sense of peaceful joy thrills and fills my soul, and one cannot understand the reason for it, because everything is so

---

[1] This letter is quoted by Mme. Dehn.

LAST PHOTOGRAPH MADE OF THE RUSSIAN ROYAL FAMILY

unutterably sad, but this comes from Above and is beside ourselves, and one knows that He will not forsake His own, will strengthen and protect."

On the day when Nicholas was brought back under guard to Tsarskoe Selo, a monarch no longer, but plain Colonel Romanoff, a great change came over Alexandra. She could not accept the Revolution as her husband did; she viewed it with uncompromising anger and contempt, but the political interests, which had been uppermost in her mind for several years, were now suddenly relegated to a subordinate plane. With an outward serenity, which amazed all those who approached her, the Empress concentrated on her family, leaving the future to God in whose goodness her faith remained unshaken. The hardships which she had to endure, and the indignities to which she was exposed, were from God ordained by His inscrutable wisdom. Each month brought a heavier burden of misfortune—she accepted it with an unflagging hope for a better future. In adversity Alexandra stood out as a noble character, while her husband remained what he was always—a very ordinary man.

Alexander Kerensky, the socialist-revolutionary member of the Duma, who had been made a member of the Provisional Government at its inception and later became Prime Minister (the Prime Minister overthrown so easily by the Bolsheviks in the autumn) went to Tsarskoe Selo to see the ex-Emperor and his family. As Minister for Justice and Procurator-General of the Senate Kerensky was responsible for the guarding, but also for the safety, of the political prisoners of the Government. M. Gilliard has told us what he knows of the incident.

Wednesday, April 4. Alexis Nicolayevitch related to me yesterday's conversation between Kerensky and the Tsar and Tsarina.

The whole family was collected in the apartment of the Grand Duchesses. Kerensky entered and introduced himself, saying:

"I am the Procurator-General, Kerensky."

Then he shook hands all round. Turning to the Tsarina, he said:

"The Queen of England asks for news of the ex-Tsarina?"

Her Majesty blushed violently. It was the first time that she had been addressed as ex-Tsarina. She answered that she was fairly well, but that her heart was troubling her as usual. Kerensky went on:

"Anything I begin I always carry through to the bitter end with all my might. I wanted to see everything myself to verify everything, so as to be able to report to Petrograd, and it will be better for you."

He then asked the Tsar to go with him into the next room as he wished to speak to him in private. He went in first and the Tsar followed. After his departure the Tsar told us that no sooner were they alone than Kerensky said to him:

"You know I've succeeded in getting the death penalty abolished? . . . I've done this in spite of the fact that a great number of my comrades have died martyrs to their convictions."

Calvary

Was he trying to make a display of his magnanimity, and insinuating that he was saving the Tsar's life though the latter had done nothing to deserve it?

He then spoke of our departure, which he still hopes to be able to arrange. When? Where? How? He did not know himself and asked that the matter should not be discussed.

It is worthy of note that Kerensky arrived at the palace in one of the Tsar's private cars driven by a chauffeur from the Imperial garage. . . .

Sunday, April 8. After Mass, Kerensky announced to the Tsar that he was obliged to separate him from the Tsarina—that he will have to live apart, only seeing Her Majesty at meals, and that on condition that only Russian is spoken. . . . A little later the Tsarina came up to me in a great state of agitation and said: "To think of his acting like this to the Tsar, playing this low trick after his self-sacrifice and his abdication to avoid civil war; how mean, how despicable. . . . A moment later she went on: "Yes, this horrible bitterness must be endured too."

I learn that Kerensky had intended at first to isolate the Tsarina, but it was pointed out to him that it would be inhuman to separate a mother from her sick children; it was then that he decided to isolate the Tsar.

To assert his authority Kerensky then arrested Anna Virubova and ordered her to be taken to St. Petersburg, but in reality his bark was more terrible than his bite. His natural kindliness made him unfit for the part of a gaoler and already on April 25 Gilliard remarks in his diary: "Kerensky's attitude towards the Tsar is no longer what it was at the beginning, he has given up his judicial bearing. . . . Kerensky has requested the papers to put an end to their campaign against the Tsar and more especially against the Tsarina. . . . He feels his responsibility towards the captives. But not a word about our departure abroad."

The Provisional Government would have liked nothing more than to be able to get rid of its embarrassing prisoners at Tsarskoe Selo by allowing them to leave for England, where they would have been taken under the protection of their royal relatives. The presence of Nicholas, so near to the capital, was a source of constant anxiety and several attempts had been made by extremists to abduct the ex-Emperor with the intention of taking him to the dungeons of the island fortress of Cronstadt, already the stronghold of the Bolsheviks. The soldiers guarding the Palace were none too reliable themselves. But the Council of Soldiers' and Workmen's Deputies created on the first day of the Revolution was becoming more powerful each day. There were in reality two Governments and the official one dared do nothing to affront its dangerous controller, the Council. So the plan for the departure of Nicholas, of Alexandra and their children could not be realized. Instead, in the middle of August, they were transferred deep into the interior, to Tobolsk in Siberia.

The diary of Nicholas for the period of his cap-

Calvary

tivity exists, or, at least, has existed in the archives in the Kremlin.[2] What we know of it bears out completely M. Gilliard's description of the captives' life within the precincts of the palace at Tsarskoe Selo [3] as not unbearable. A régime was gradually established which, apart from the visits of a not unfriendly commandant, left them free to do as they liked within their private apartments and they had a part of the park in which they could walk and indulge in the pleasures of gardening. The soldiers guarding them had lost their original discipline, but had not evolved yet into the dissolute ruffians they became a year later. They were coarse in their expressions and at times aggressive—they took away from Alexis the toy gun with which he played in the garden—but they meant no real harm and could usually be disarmed by a joke or a smile. The officers in command were mostly decent fellows, they went in fear of their own men, but, when they could, they did all in their power to help the captives. A number of servants in the palace remained faithful to their old masters and carried out their duties as well as possible. The Government made a sufficient allowance for maintenance and, although visitors from outside were not permitted, it was possible to send and receive letters with comparative ease.

---

[2] The diary is known to us by extracts published by a man who worked in the archives and later escaped abroad: *Sovremmenmiya Sapisky*, XIV, 1923, Paris.

[3] It should be noted that the name Tsarskoe Selo, which can be translated as: Czar's Village, originated really in the Finnish word "Saari" (island), as before the conquest by Peter the Great its population was Finnish.

The Tragic Bride

There was no restriction on newspapers and books and, gradually, as Kerensky became accustomed to his charges, the régime was relaxed, provided, always, that the suspicions of the Council of Soldiers' and Workmen's Deputies were not awakened.

From the diary of Nicholas we discover that, when he returned to Tsarskoe Selo after his abdication, he busied himself with the burning of a large number of letters and other documents. This does not indicate a close surveillance during that period. Afterwards when things had settled down a bit, Nicholas and Alexandra turned their attention to the education of their son. The Emperor became responsible for history and geography, while the Empress, characteristically, took charge of religious instruction. The chief pleasure was walking in the park, felling trees and tending the kitchen garden laid out by the combined effort of the whole family. The Empress, whose health was not good, usually was taken out by her husband in a wheeled chair and placed in a sunny spot on the lawn, while her boy was playing near her. It was then that two soldiers came to take away the toy gun with which Alexis was happily playing. The proud Empress refrained from speaking to the men and asked Gilliard, who was near, to intervene, while she patted the sobbing child. . . . In a letter smuggled out and dated June 5 Alexandra writes:

> . . . I am remembering the past. It is necessary to look more calmly on everything. What is to be done? Once He sent us such trials, evidently He

thinks we are sufficiently prepared for it. It is a sort of examination—it is necessary to prove that we did not go through it in vain. One can find in everything something good and useful—whatever sufferings we go through—let it be, He will give us force and patience and will not leave us. He is merciful. It is only necessary to bow to His wish without murmur and await —there on the other side He is preparing to all who love Him indescribable joy. . . . I believe strongly the bad will pass and there will be a clear and cloudless sky. . . . One must have a little patience—and is it really so difficult? For every day that passes quietly I thank God. . . . Three months have passed now. The people were promised that they would have more food and fuel, but all has become worse and more expensive. They have deceived everybody—I am so sorry for them. How many we have helped but now it is all finished. . . .

It must have been a terrible day for the Empress when from the newspapers, which were supplied freely to the Palace, she learned that a number of soldiers had opened the tomb of Rasputin and had taken away the coffin to an unknown destination. It transpired later that the body of the "Man of God" had been burnt on a great bonfire in a forest several miles away from Tsarskoe Selo and the ashes had been scattered in the wind. The icons deposited on the tomb by the Empress and her daughters were taken away by the soldiery and sold for a few roubles to collectors.

Another tragic day was May the first, when a

267

noisy procession bearing red banners with incendiary inscriptions marched through the park and in full view of the Palace a grave was prepared in which with much speechifying several "victims" of the Revolution were buried for the edification of the populace.

After five months of detention it was decided to remove Nicholas from the neighbourhood of the capital. The Council of Soldiers' and Workmen's Deputies was told by the Provisional Government that this was necessary to make any attempt at liberation more difficult, but in reality it was desired to protect the captive family who were becoming daily more in danger. On August twelfth—the birthday of Alexis, who was now thirteen—Nicholas was warned to be ready to leave for an unknown destination by midnight. At the appointed hour the captives, excited by sudden departure, were dressed ready for travel and with their luggage packed to be taken away. Hours passed without anything happening. Kerensky arrived bringing the Grand Duke Michael, who had been permitted to say good-bye to his brother. But yet there was no train. It transpired that the Union of Railwaymen had become suspicious and refused to allow the train to leave. The Government in its powerlessness started to negotiate and at last, after five in the morning, the resistance of the Union was broken. The ex-Imperial family was taken by motor car to a neighbouring small station and put aboard a waiting train, which, guarded by a special detachment, set itself in motion eastwards: it was to take the captives to Siberia. Exhausted by hours of waiting they were too sleepy to pay much attention to Kerensky who had come to see them off and with kind words tried to reassure them on their fate. Did he foresee that in a few weeks his position would not be more enviable than that of Nicholas? That soon he himself would be deposed?

It seldom happens—and it is well so—that a human being, predestined to a cruel end can see beyond the nearest stage of the road. For Nicholas and his family the days passed in the comfortable sleeping car, which carried them towards Siberia, were a pleasing interlude in the monotony of their existence as captives. But in the purring song of the smoothly running train we hear the jarring rumble of the tumbril carrying its victims to execution.

When Alexandra learnt that their destination was the town of Tobolsk, not far from Pokrovskoye, the village of her friend, she must have been impressed. In days gone by, in those intimate talks she enjoyed so much, Rasputin had told her about his native country: its great rivers, virgin forests, beautiful flowers and balsamic air. He had promised that some day she would see it all, and now it was going to happen. The "Man of God" had said that the fate of the dynasty was inextricably united with his own. The approach to his birthplace, was it an omen? And if so, good or bad? The train, meanwhile, was running eastwards and on the evening of the third day the town of Tioumen was reached. It lies beyond the Urals, in Asia, on the bank of the broad Irtish river. In the sixteenth century the Cossacks came down it in their frail boats to conquer Siberia for the Moscow Czars. Here was the gateway through which bands of adventurers poured into the eastern wilderness, seeking lands to conquer and tribes to put to ransom, pressing onwards and reaching the shores of the Pacific, thousands of miles away, in less than eighty years. Not far from here on the banks of the Irtish stood Iskor, the capital of a great Tartar State, which the legendary Yermack with a few hundred followers—a Muscovite Cortez—took and destroyed.

Siberia became the land from which the Czars obtained fabulous riches and to which they exiled their victims. The Russian people in their thousands poured into it to make it the granary and the cattle reserve of the Empire and to extract its natural wealth. Year in, year out Siberia had sent priceless tribute to the Court of Russian sovereigns, but to Alexandra from it came a fatal gift—Rasputin. At Tioumen the Imperial family was placed on board a steamer which took them down river. Soon on the bank they discovered the wooden buildings of the village in which the "Man of God" had been born and where the large stone house he had built stood out as a landmark. Alexandra was on deck, looking ardently towards the place. Gilliard remarks in his diary that there was nothing to surprise her in this event which Rasputin had foretold and chance, once more, seemed to confirm his prophetic words. Two days later, when the steamer rounded a bend, the ancient citadel of Tobolsk was discovered on its high mound. Like many other Russian towns, Tobolsk, imposing to look at from a distance, is poor and mean inside and has no accommodation to offer to strangers. The Imperial party was kept waiting on board for several days until the Governor's House, the only suitable building, was prepared to receive them. This was the first real change from the conditions of Tsarskoe Selo. Instead of their comfortable apartments the family were confined to a few rooms in an indifferent state of repair and poorly furnished, while the sanitary arrangements were so bad that there was constantly a disagreeable smell from the drains. There was no park to walk in, no garden even, only a narrow yard, enclosed with a high wall and overlooked by the barracks in which the soldiers, who watched the prisoners, were lodged. Otherwise the conditions of captivity were the same as before. The Commandant of the Guard, a colonel of the old army, was more than kind and refrained from interfering in the inner arrangements. But after a few weeks two commissioners arrived, sent by Kerensky to prevent the Council of Soldiers' and Workmen's Deputies from accusing the Government of weakness. These men were old Revolutionaries, who under the Imperial régime had suffered long terms of imprisonment and had then been exiled to a distant province in Siberia. One of them was quite a decent fellow and, after a time, became quite attached to the children, but the other was a narrow doctrinaire, soured by the miseries endured and full of rancour. He did his utmost to make the life of the captives resemble what he had passed through himself. "Now it's their turn" was his refrain, when remonstrated with on the subject of some new petty annoyance he had invented.

For Nicholas and especially for Alexandra, a question of primordial importance was that of the religious services. They were not satisfied with the permission for a priest, accompanied by a deacon, to celebrate service in the house itself. As there was no consecrated altar Holy Mass could not be celebrated. After long negotiations in which the authorities in St. Petersburg had to intervene, the prisoners were allowed to go every Sunday to a church, which was separated from the Governor's House by a public garden. The inhabitants of Tobolsk, unaffected yet by the revolutionary spirit, showed such marked respect for the ex-Emperor that it was found necessary to close the church to the public. The commissioners stationed guards to prevent all intercourse and even forbade the inhabitants to stand anywhere near the house. The guards were instructed to prevent people from standing in view of the windows and showing their respect for the fallen Monarch by making the sign of the Cross.

The detachment which guarded the prisoners was composed of soldiers from Tsarskoe Selo. Among them were several decent fellows, but the majority were already influenced by an insidious propaganda.

As time went on their attitude towards the prisoners became more truculent. So, just out of spite, they destroyed one day the snow mountain, which had been erected in the yard to amuse the children. The pretext was that Nicholas and Alexandra had gone to the top of it to look over the fencing. A much more tragic thing happened on Christmas Day. The prisoners had been allowed to go to church, where after Mass the old deacon from a lifelong habit intoned the prayer for the long life of the Imperial family. The soldiers present interrupted the service and threatened to kill priest and deacon then and there. Another painful incident occurred when the soldiers demanded that the ex-Emperor should remove the epaulettes from his uniform. Gilliard relates that "at first it seemed that the Tsar would refuse, but after exchanging a look and a few words with the Tsarina, he recovered self-control and yielded for the sake of his family."

Alexandra preserved her wonderful calm through all this trying time. She wrote in a letter, which escaped the censor, March 2:

> . . . We hope to do our devotions next week if we are allowed to do so. I am looking forward to those beautiful services—such a longing to pray in church. I dream of our church and of my little cell-like corner near the altar. Nature is beautiful, everything is shining and brilliantly lighted up. . . . I relive in mind, day by day, through the year that has passed and think of those I saw for the last time. . . . We cannot

complain, we have got everything, we live well, thanks to the touching kindness of the people, who in secret send us bread, fish, pies, etc.

Do not worry about us, darling beloved one. For you all it is hard and, especially, for our Country. . . .[4]

All one's feelings have been trampled underfoot, but so it has to be, the soul must grow and rise above all else; that which is most dear and tender in us has been wounded, is it not true? So we too have to understand through it all that God is greater than everything and that He wants to draw us, through our sufferings, closer to Him. Love him more and better than one and all . . . help will come from Above, people can no longer do anything, but with God all things are possible, and He will show His strength, wisdom and all forgiveness and love. . . .

There was a thing, however, which upset Alexandra. It was the news in the newspapers about further successes of the Germans or further concessions to them on the part of the Government. She had never been friendly to official Germany, but now she hated it because she could not forgive William II for having sanctioned the unnatural alliance between his General Staff and the Bolsheviks. The treaty of Brest-Litovsk filled her with intense loathing for a nation, which for material advantage could agree to compromise with the enemies of civilization. It is

---

[4] This quotation is taken, as the preceding ones in this chapter, from the book of Mme. L. Dehn, a friend of the Empress: *The Real Tsaritsa.*

not impossible that this intense dislike for Germany may have been in the way, when plans of escape were discussed. The soldiers on guard were undisciplined and careless, as was proved by the fact that letters and parcels were constantly passing in and out. Bold partisans had on repeated occasions made plans for the escape of Nicholas and even of the whole family and there is little doubt that facilities were offered from the German side for crossing the frontier. But Nicholas and Alexandra insisted on two conditions which made matters complicated: they refused to be separated and would not leave Russia. Gilliard relates that the Empress told him, when discussing the possibility of escape:

"I wouldn't leave Russia on any consideration, for it seems to me that to go abroad would be to break our last link with the past, which would then be dead for ever."

On another occasion she said in a low voice, full of suppressed feeling:

"After what they have done to the Tsar, I would rather die in Russia than be saved by the Germans."

In the winter of 1918, when the Bolsheviks had not yet established themselves within the country it would have been practicable to arrange for the escape. But if there were any serious attempts in that direction—and personally we are not sure that there were any—invaluable time was lost in discussions and hesitation and then it was too late. Gilliard remarks in his diary under March 23:

The Tragic Bride

"Our last chance of escape has been snatched from us."

A detachment of Red Guards arrived on that day as a garrison for Tobolsk. The soldiers of the old Guard, bad though they were themselves, resented their presence and would not permit the Commissar, who was at their head, to enter the Governor's House and see the prisoners. But a peremptory demand was received by the Commandant from the Soviet Government ordering him to submit and to introduce a much stricter régime for the prisoners. Until then some of the persons who had followed the family to Tobolsk had been allowed to live in town but now they were brought to the House and treated as prisoners also. A few days later the supreme disaster occurred: Alexis, whose health had been remarkably good all the time, now suddenly was taken with severe pains: an attack of his disease—haemophilia. A few days later arrived a Commissar with extraordinary powers from the central Government. As far as one can judge it was the intention of Lenin at that time to have Nicholas brought to Moscow either to stand his trial for treason, or to be delivered to Germany. But things turned out not exactly as planned. On April 25, the Commissar informed Nicholas that his orders were to take him away from Tobolsk immediately. If any members of the family wanted to accompany him they could do so. But Alexis was prostrated with his pains and could not be moved. Gilliard, the faithful chronicler, tells us that Alexandra sent for him and speaking as to a friend of the family she let him see what was in her mind. She was greatly upset, for once her calm had forsaken her and she walked up and down the room, talking rather to herself than to Gilliard. What she feared most was to allow Nicholas to go without her. For she suspected the Government of a desire to extort from him some unseemly confession.

". . . I can't let the Tsar go alone. They want to separate him from his family as they did before . . . they're going to try to force his hand . . . the Tsar is necessary to them; they feel that he alone represents Russia . . . together we shall be in a better position to resist them . . . but the boy is still so ill . . . for the first time in my life I do not know what to do. . . ."

Then at last she told Gilliard:

"Yes, that will be best; I'll go with the Tsar; I shall trust Alexis to you. . . ."

So it was decided that Alexandra and her third daughter Marie would accompany Nicholas, while the other members of the family would remain with the stricken child. The little band of devoted friends and servants went about the house ready to break down with grief. But Alexandra had regained her serenity and her steadfast faith inspired her husband and all the others. On the next morning there was a pathetic leavetaking. During the seven months passed at Tobolsk the relations between Nicholas and Alexandra and the few people who were allowed to share their captivity had become very intimate, not as between masters and servants but as between friends and even relatives. When they were all powerful Nicholas and Alexandra obtained service by dispensing favours, now they were given it for love alone. The endurance of Alexandra had reached the breaking point. In the room above, her sick child was weeping wildly and crying: "Mother, mother." She hastened into the street, where peasant carts were waiting to take the prisoners on the next stage of their dolorous journey, for the steamers had not yet been able to resume their service. A Siberian cart is an instrument of torture. It consists of a wicker basket hung between two long parallel poles which serve as springs. The passenger squats or lies on the bottom of the basket. To accomplish several scores of miles over heavy roads is martyrdom, especially for a woman in indifferent health as was Alexandra. The strong little horses rush at great speed while the carriage bounces and flings itself from side to side and sometimes upsets completely. This happened to the cart in which was the poor Empress as she notes in her diary. As it was impossible to reach Tioumen in one day the night was passed in Pokrovskoye, the village of Rasputin. Alexandra had the satisfaction of seeing the family of her Friend for a moment at the window of their house. At Tioumen the party was put on board a train, which started westwards. The Commissar declared that their destination was Moscow. But at Yekaterinenburg, the capital of the Urals, the provincial Soviet ordered the prisoners to be removed from the train. They were placed in a dirty motor lorry, which, jarring and rumbling over the rough cobblestones, took them to the house of a certain Ipatieff, who was turned out to make room for the new inhabitants. A month later the rest of the family was brought from Tobolsk to Yekaterinenburg but Gilliard was not allowed to accompany them. This circumstance to which he owed his life, deprives us of an eyewitness and we have to rely for further details on what is known to us of the diaries of Nicholas and Alexandra.

Tobolsk had been much worse than Tsarskoe Selo, but compared with Yekaterinenburg it was Paradise. For now the Imperial family found itself in a real prison. All relations with the world outside were cut off. The prisoners were put on scanty rations and were allowed exercise only for one hour a day in the small garden attached to the house. The panes in the windows were painted a dull white and in the whole place only one window could be opened so that during the hot weather in May and June the fetid air inside the rooms often reached a temperature of eighty degrees Fahrenheit. The prisoners suffered very much and the boy Alexis most of all: he lost weight and looked emaciated. There were not sufficient beds and the grand duchesses slept on mattresses on the floor. The health of Alexandra got worse. Her heart troubled her and feeling weak she remained whole days in bed. The exercise in the garden in the presence of insolent Red guardsmen presented no attraction for her. She preferred for hours to read the Bible and to meditate. Her diary mentions often that she "gathered her thoughts." But we find in it also the enumeration of the few pleasures, which on rare occasions were permitted to the prisoners. So one day the children were delighted to receive a fruit salad and on another a kind Red passed to them some chocolate. Gradually the few servants who remained with the family were removed. The last to go was the faithful sailor Nagorny the "nurse" of Alexis. The grand duchesses bravely did all the housework. They dusted, polished, did the washing and even managed to bake bread, a feat commented upon by Nicholas in his diary. In July the conditions became worse. The infamous Yuroffsky was appointed Commissar and instituted a system of regular searches. He deprived the prisoners of their milk ration and confiscated all the jewellery they had in their possession. He even tried to wrench off Nicholas' wedding ring, but after nearly twenty-five years it refused to come off. The approach of civil war to Yekaterinenburg created a state of nervous tension among the Reds, which obliged the prisoners to give up their hour of exercise, so as to avoid hearing the filthy and impudent comments of their gaolers. In the second week of

July, Alexis had a new attack of bleeding and lay with a high temperature, but his distracted mother could not obtain permission to call a doctor. Cut off from the world, suffocating in the bad air of the unventilated rooms, badly nourished and constantly exposed to the insults of their tyrants the prisoners fell a prey to melancholy. Sometimes they tried their hand at a game of bézique and the Empress found a sheet anchor in the reading of the Bible. . . .[5]

"In that day will I raise the tabernacle of David that is fallen." The Empress meditates these words of the prophet Amos, which she has just heard. It is not far from midnight. The air in the room is warm and stuffy. Alexandra cannot sleep. She has laid her weary body on the hard couch and is listening to the calm breathing of her husband and to the agitated one of her boy. Poor dear child: he is not at all well, he is feverish, to-morrow morning Alexandra must try again to obtain from the Commissar the permission for the doctor to see Alexis. "I will

---

[5] The above details of the detention of the Imperial family at Yekaterinenburg are based on the extracts known to us from the diaries of Nicholas and Alexandra. The only discrepancy which we can discover is in the question of the doctor and the servants. The ultimate fate of the family was shared by Dr. Botkin, Demidova— the maid of the Empress, Kharitonoff—a cook, Troup—a footman and in addition there was Sednieff—a scullery boy, whose life was spared. This is in contradiction to the statement in the diaries that the family was deprived of their servants and that the doctor was not allowed to approach the sick Alexis. The contradiction is probably only apparent and exposes the cruelty of the gaolers, who evidently, forbade the doctor to leave his room and the servants to render aid to the grand duchesses. But what does a detail like this matter in the presence of the final tragedy?

raise the tabernacle of David that is fallen." Yes, Alexandra believes in Providence. The pact with heaven stands and all will be well. All must be well. The sufferings are from God . . . but oh how difficult it is to suffer and not to lose hope sometimes. Miracles happen. Did not God help to soften the heart of the terrible Avdieff, the drunken brutish Commissar, who began by being so beastly? Was not his heart touched? Did he not become friendly? And Moshkin, his fierce assistant? Did he not pass to Nicky that letter from outside promising help? It is true they were denounced to the Soviet and Yuroffsky, the cruel man, was sent to replace them. But faith works miracles. Perhaps even he? . . . one must only believe, wait and pray.

Steps in the corridor. The door to the room in which Nicholas, Alexandra, and their son were sleeping is flung open. Yuroffsky enters and summons everybody to rise immediately: there are disturbances in town, the prisoners will have to leave immediately; they must dress and assemble in a room below. Yuroffsky is in a hurry and gives the prisoners barely time to put on their clothes and snatch a few belongings. He leads them downstairs. Nicholas comes first with his eyes yet filled with sleep and carrying his son in his arms, Alexandra follows with the daughters and behind them guards push forward the old Dr. Botkin, Anna Demidova, the maid, who is carrying a pile of cushions; Kharitonoff, the old *chef* from Tsarskoe Selo, and Troup, the valet.

282

Calvary

The prisoners are herded into the room indicated by Yuroffsky. It is a cellar really, lighted by one unshaded bulb. The carriages to take them away have not yet come, says Yuroffsky. He goes out to see about them. There are three chairs. Alexis, who cannot stand because of his leg, sinks down on one. Near him sits the ex-Emperor. His wife has pushed her chair to the wall against which she leans her weary head. The others stand, sagging sleepily against the walls for support. Minutes pass. Yuroffsky comes in again. With him are others. He goes up to Nicholas and shouts: "Your men have tried to save you but haven't succeeded, and we are forced to put you to death." His revolver is in his hand, he fires point-blank and Nicholas collapses. Yuroffsky then shoots the boy. The other assassins meanwhile with a fusillade of shots have dispatched the rest of the prisoners. Anna, the maid, has escaped the bullets and makes a rush for the door. The assassins throw themselves upon her and stab her to death with their bayonets. The boy lies on the floor feebly moaning. Yuroffsky puts a bullet into his head. One of the grand duchesses is not quite dead and is also finished off with the bayonet. Pools of blood are forming. The plaster of the walls is pitted by the bullets and shows gashes from wildly swung bayonets. The assassins proceed to search the dead. . . . A motor lorry is at the entrance, The bodies are dragged to it and thrown in anyhow. The lorry drives away into the night, jarring and rumbling over the rough cobblestones. The way leads into the forest, where near a disused mineshaft the materials for a bonfire have been prepared. The bodies are burnt and the ashes are thrown down the shaft. Another insensate crime will go down into history. . . .[6]

[6] The scene of the murder has been reconstructed from the facts discovered by the Commission of Inquiry, which after the advance of the White armies, was able soon after to proceed with its work with such good effect that three men who were present at the assasination were discovered and interrogated. Their evidence as well as that of other important witnesses forms several volumes.

CHAPTER XIX

THE VICTIM

HE assassins, when they threw the bodies of Nicholas and Alexandra into the fire and then flung the mingled ashes down the pit, could not suspect that they were complying with a dear wish of their victims.

"No more separations. At last united, bound for life, and, when this life is ended, to meet together in the other world to remain together for all eternity."

These words Alix wrote in her husband's diary during their honeymoon. She would not have spoken otherwise on the day of her death. If given the choice she would have preferred to die with her beloved, sharing his nameless grave, than to outlive him and lie alone in a rich tomb. Her life was great indeed and deserved to endure, when earthly links were broken. Death had no terror for her. During the Revolution she said:

"I cannot understand any one being afraid to die. I have always looked upon Death as such a friend, such a rest."

Her murderers did not know how to be cruel. If

285

they had, they would have let Alix live. . . . The world has said, and many continue to hold the view, that the Empress's mind was concentrated on political power, that to satisfy her ambition in this respect she was ready to sacrifice even her family. The faults committed by her are so glaring and their results have been so tragic that it is difficult to say a word in her defence. We hope, however, that this book will help to dispel the false view about her ambition. When Nicholas returned, after having abdicated, his wife saw autocracy, the splendid castle of her dreams, brought down and become as dust. It would have been natural for her to bewail the loss and recriminate. Instead, she called Nicholas her "hero" and assured him that it was not as Emperor that he was cherished, but as lover, husband, and father.

The political ambition of Alix was the fruit of her desire to see Nicholas go down in history as a great monarch. Affairs of State would not have interested her, if they had not formed such an important part in the life of her husband. It was Nicholas himself who drew her into an active association with him in his political work. Alix would never have tried herself to rule, if, at a critical moment, she had not discovered the weakness of Nicholas. She was governed not by ambition, but by a sense of duty towards her husband and her son. Her attempt to save autocracy failed. It hastened the final catastrophe. The ideas of the Empress were wrong; her methods were wrong likewise. During her lifetime she was punished already

by the terrible accusations which were levelled at her
and which could not be stilled. But Russia has not
the right of considering itself the victim of Alix. It
was the latter who was the victim of Russia.

The fate of the granddaughter of Queen Victoria
was shaped by two men: Nicholas and Rasputin. Both
were typical Russian products. The unsatisfactory
Emperor was the fruit of a régime, which, while it
prostituted the will and conscience of its people, reduced also the moral stature of its rulers. What
guidance could come from Nicholas? Because Alix
loved him, because she loved him so much, she ideal-
ized him and was drawn down to his mental level,
where tradition stood in front of reason and preconceived notions came before logical conclusions. The
granddaughter of the Prince Consort, who was a
statesman, and of Queen Victoria, who understood
the balance of duty and privilege, became the wife of
a man who was convinced of the divine origin of his
title and who was not a politician, much less a statesman. The daughter of the Princess Alice of Great
Britain, to whom Strauss had dedicated his *Life of Voltaire,* was married to a man who believed that the
best place for philosophers was in prison. Alix
adopted the views of Nicholas and, as often happens,
the gifted pupil overtook and surpassed the master.
After the period of reforms of Alexander II the
Romanoffs in the following generation had relapsed
and had gone back to the comfortable formula: Autocracy, Orthodoxy and Nationality, which permitted

them to resist democratic demands. Alix accepted the formula with enthusiasm. She believed that autocracy, instituted by the pact with heaven, was of divine origin and the only form of government suitable for Russia. The pact had been made with the Orthodox Church, as the representative of God on earth. Thus autocracy and Orthodoxy interpenetrated each other, forming one whole. The Empress, therefore, held the view that the Orthodox could not be Republicans. The only nationality to which true Russians could belong, was the one which accepted autocracy and practised Orthodoxy. The deplorable result of these fallacies we have seen. But it was the influence of Rasputin, which was the real disaster.

The spiritual origin of Rasputin, like that of Tolstoy and Lenin, is to be found in the peculiar quality of the Russian Slav, which urges him to oppose established authority, whether it be that of the Church, of the Government, or of society. Opposition does not go as a rule beyond a state of chronic discontent, expressed by biting criticism, but kept in leash by a no less typical reluctance to pass from words to action. At times, however, the spirit of opposition overcomes all existing checks and indulges in an orgy of destruction. Russian Bolshevism is above all destructive and posterity will remember Lenin as the destroyer of all things. For his claim to be a builder does not go beyond the fact that he tried to destroy scientifically. Tolstoy too, when considered apart from his literary genius and his personal goodness, was a destroyer.

The Victim

He attacked existing social conditions with conspicuous success. But the doctrine of non-resistance, which he patronized, can hardly be called constructive. A Russian poet appealed to his countrymen to build rationally for eternity. Tolstoy had no objection to seeing all buildings levelled with the ground and would have liked to have a plough pass over the whole. Rasputin was a destroyer. He attacked the moral foundations of society and his sinister power was all the greater, because he acted unconsciously, urged by a devilish impulse. The Empress was his unwitting tool; she imagined that she was building solidly for the future. This was a tragic thing, but her whole life in Russia had been a tragedy from the day, when as a bride she came to the man she loved. A tragic fate held her in its grip. No wonder she was ready to welcome death as the deliverer. . . .

In more fortunate circumstances she would have been a charming and lovable personality. In flashes her charm appeared even under uncongenial conditions. We cannot resist the pleasure of telling the following story, which illustrates our meaning. At the height of the Revolution, when there was no news from the Emperor and when mutinous soldiers were gathering round the Palace, a lady devoted to the Empress offered to sleep on a couch near her bedroom. Collecting sheets and blankets the lady began to prepare her bed. The Empress came in in her nightdress, over which she had thrown a dressing gown. With her long hair in a heavy plait falling down her back she looked girlish, but her face belied this impression, so pale was it, so ethereal, so pathetic. She looked at the clumsy heap of the bedclothes and an affectionate, mocking smile softened suddenly the tightly drawn lips: "You ladies don't know how to be useful. When I was a girl, my grandmother, Queen Victoria, showed me how to make a bed, I'll teach you." Poor Empress, during the weary days of her imprisonment she often must have gone back in her memory to the Granny of her youth.

The Soviet czars of the Lenin dynasty did not feel secure in the Kremlin until they had put to death the last representative of the line they had displaced. Tyrant eats tyrant. But Democracy looks upon the Yekaterinenburg murders not only with loathing, but with a feeling of bitter regret. For the seed is sown of future reaction. Through Bolshevik folly monarchism has found its martyrs.

INDEX

Index

Index

Index

294

Index

Index

Index

Index

Index

(1)

THE END